MICHAEL WILSON

AIO: The New SEO – How to Get Your Business Found by AI

A Step-by-Step Guide for Business Owners to Dominate Visibility in the Era of AI

First edition

This book was professionally typeset on Reedsy.
Find out more at reedsy.com

Contents

1 Chapter 1: The Rise of AI as the New Search Layer 1
2 Chapter 2: Understanding AIO (AI Optimization) 13
3 Chapter 3: Building an AI-Optimized Content Strategy 21
4 Chapter 4: Becoming an Authority in the AI Ecosystem 35
5 Chapter 5: Structuring Your Website for AIO 46
6 Chapter 6: Leveraging Other Platforms to Boost AI Visibility 56
7 Chapter 7: AI Tools That Can Help You Optimize for AI 64
8 Chapter 8: Creating Your Own AI Entity 76
9 Chapter 9: Tracking & Measuring AIO Success 84
10 Chapter 10: Future-Proofing Your Business in the AI Era 93
11 AIO checklist 100
12 Prompt Library: Content Optimization with ChatGPT 103
13 AIO Audit Worksheet 106
14 Glossary of AIO Terms 110

1

Chapter 1: The Rise of AI as the New Search Layer

How people are using ChatGPT and other LLMs to search for businesses and solutions

The way people search for information is changing quickly. In the past, they would go to Google, type in a few keywords, and click through a list of links. That process relied heavily on traditional search engine optimization. Businesses competed to earn top spots on search results, knowing that visibility on the first page often led to traffic, leads, and sales. Today, something different is happening. People are turning to AI tools like ChatGPT, Claude, Gemini, and Perplexity to get straight answers to their questions. These platforms are not just changing how people find information. They are reshaping how customers discover businesses, make decisions, and solve problems.

Instead of typing fragmented keywords into a search bar, users now speak to these AI platforms in full, natural sentences. They ask specific questions and expect specific answers. When someone wants to know which CRM is best for their business, where to find a reliable private lender, or how to automate their client onboarding, they are no longer starting with a Google search. They are asking ChatGPT. This behavior reflects a deeper change in how people interact with technology. They are no longer willing to sift through dozens of websites to find what they need. They want fast, clear, and personalized answers.

People are using these AI tools to get recommendations, compare services, understand complex topics, and discover tools or professionals they can trust. A business owner might ask, "What are the best platforms for hosting a paid membership community?" or "Who are the top coaches helping veterans start businesses?" Instead of pointing to a list of websites, the AI gives a synthesized answer that combines insights from many sources. If your business is not included in that response, the user may never hear about you, even if your offer is a perfect fit.

The speed and convenience of these tools are part of their appeal. They remove the noise. A user no longer has to open five tabs, read through outdated blogs, or scroll past ads just to get to the point. ChatGPT and similar platforms deliver what the user needs in one answer. If the user wants more details, they ask a follow-up question, and the AI responds instantly. This conversation-style search is far more efficient and engaging than the old way of browsing through results.

This is especially important for service providers and local businesses. People are asking for recommendations for attorneys, dentists, real estate agents, and consultants based on specific needs. They want to know who understands their situation and who they can trust. Someone might ask, "What are the best real estate agents for military families relocating to Texas?" or "Where can I find a financial advisor who understands the needs of veterans?" The AI tools scan available data and respond with suggestions. If your business shows up in that answer, you gain trust immediately. If you are not mentioned, you miss the opportunity altogether.

We are also seeing professionals use these tools as private advisors. Business owners ask how to build a sales funnel, price their services, or structure their offers. Coaches and consultants ask how to craft their messaging or set up automated workflows. Entrepreneurs ask what tech stack is best for scaling their brand. These are high-value questions that used to require research, webinars, or consulting sessions. Now they are being asked directly to AI assistants. The businesses that are mentioned in the answers benefit from instant visibility and authority.

People are also using these tools for product discovery. Instead of searching for "best gifts for entrepreneurs" and browsing ten blog posts, they simply ask ChatGPT and get a curated list in seconds. If your product is referenced in those results, you get exposure. If not, you are invisible to the user. These AI tools are influencing decisions in real time, across every industry and niche.

Even hiring decisions are being shaped by AI. Users ask, "What are the best platforms to find a ghostwriter?" or "Who are the most recommended business coaches for introverts?" These questions generate lists, comparisons, and summaries that guide the user's choice. The AI pulls from online reviews, content, and other digital signals. If your presence online is strong and well-positioned, the AI may recommend you. If your messaging is unclear, inconsistent, or hidden behind generic language, you may be passed over.

People trust these AI answers because they are fast, simple, and feel personal. There is a growing confidence in the results generated by tools like ChatGPT. In many cases, users will not verify the response with additional searches. They are taking the answer at face value. That means you only get one chance to be included in that answer. Your business must be visible, your content must be clear, and your expertise must be positioned in a way that AI tools can recognize.

The information these platforms use is not pulled from live Google searches. It comes from training data, public websites, structured content, and sometimes integrated plugins. This means you need to think differently about where your content shows up. Are you featured on platforms like Medium, Substack, Quora, or LinkedIn? Are you mentioned in online reviews or public directories? Do you publish content that explains your services in a way AI can understand? These questions are at the heart of visibility in the AI-powered world.

Let's say you run a consulting firm for small business automation. If someone asks ChatGPT, "How do I automate my service business to save time?" the AI may provide a strategy and mention tools, software, or experts. If your name, business, or content has been published in the right places and framed with clarity, you may be included in that answer. If not, someone else will take your spot. It is not about who is the best. It is about who is the most visible and clearly defined.

This shift means your authority must be digital and distributed. Having a good website is not enough. You need to be active on the platforms that AI tools learn from. You need to provide value through educational content, share your expertise in Q&A forums, and publish insights that establish your position in your market. AI platforms are trained to recognize authority, clarity, and consistency. Your job is to give them what they need to trust and recommend you.

Consumers are no longer clicking their way through the internet. They are talking their way to answers. Every question they ask is an opportunity for your business to be discovered, trusted, and chosen. If you understand how these tools work and how people use them, you can shape your strategy to align with this new behavior. You can write content that answers questions clearly, publish material where it counts, and show up with purpose.

This is the future of business visibility. The way people find solutions has changed. They are asking questions, not typing keywords. They are having conversations, not scrolling through ads. If you want to grow your brand, attract clients, and stand out in a crowded market, you need to show up where the conversation is happening. You need to optimize your presence so that when AI platforms deliver answers, your business is included.

The companies that adapt to this now will dominate attention in the years ahead. They will earn trust quickly, generate leads without cold outreach, and become known as the go-to experts in their space. People are searching differently. They are looking for confidence, clarity, and convenience. Be the business that gives them all three. Be the answer.

Key differences between traditional search engines and LLM-based tools

Understanding the difference between traditional search engines and large language model-based tools like ChatGPT, Claude, and Gemini is one of the most important steps for any business owner looking to gain visibility in today's digital world. These platforms may seem similar on the surface since both help people find information, but the way they work, what they prioritize, and how they deliver results are entirely different. If you want to grow your brand and remain competitive, you need to know how each of these systems functions and how they influence what people see.

Traditional search engines rely on crawling, indexing, and ranking websites across the internet. They look at hundreds of signals to decide which content to show for a given query. These include keyword density, domain authority, backlinks, load speed, mobile responsiveness, and user behavior. The goal is to deliver a ranked list of relevant websites the user can click on and explore. In this environment, content creators play a game of optimizing every technical piece of the puzzle to try and land a spot on the first page. The more optimized your site, the more likely you were to be seen.

Large language model-based tools like ChatGPT, on the other hand, do not present a list of links. They provide a direct answer, written in a conversational tone, generated from a combination of their training data and retrieval systems. When a person types a question into ChatGPT, the response they get is not pulled from a single website. It is synthesized from knowledge the AI has learned during training and, in some cases, pulled from a database of trusted content. The answer is presented in plain language, often with step-by-step detail, offering immediate value. This completely changes the search experience.

Instead of clicking through multiple links, users now get a single, refined answer within seconds. That answer might include comparisons, instructions, definitions, or recommendations. In many cases, users never need to visit a website at all. They get what they came for right there in the conversation. This makes large language models extremely efficient and user-friendly, especially for people who want fast answers and minimal decision fatigue.

One of the most noticeable differences between the two systems lies in how they prioritize content. Traditional search engines rely heavily on popularity and optimization. The more backlinks you have, the better you rank. The more your content aligns with keywords, the more visible you become. These algorithms can be manipulated. In fact, entire industries were built around helping businesses game the system. Large language models do not operate on those same rules. Instead of focusing on links and keyword density, they prioritize clarity, relevance, and language structure. They are not measuring how many people link to your page. They are evaluating how well your content explains a topic, how helpful it is, and whether it aligns with the question being asked.

This shift changes what kind of content performs well. While long-form content still has value, it now needs to be written in a way that feels more like a helpful guide than a keyword-stuffed article. The AI is looking for clear explanations, natural tone, and well-structured answers. It favors content that sounds like a real person talking to another person. That means if you are used to writing for search engines, you need to adjust your voice. The content that succeeds in this new environment is content that serves, teaches, and communicates.

The trust dynamic is also different. In traditional search, users decide which result they want to trust. They look at the brand, the design of the site, reviews, and how well the page answers their question. In an AI-based interaction, users are putting their trust in the platform itself. If ChatGPT or Claude gives them an answer, they are more likely to accept it without double-checking. That means if your business is mentioned in the response, you benefit from a transfer of credibility. People trust you because the AI mentioned you. On the other hand, if you are not included, you may never be considered, even if your business is the best option available.

Another key difference is how each system handles updates and real-time content. Search engines regularly crawl the internet for new content and can index changes within hours or days. You can publish a blog post or update your services page and potentially see traffic right away. Large language models are different. Some are trained on static datasets that are not updated in real time. Others, like ChatGPT with browsing or plugin capabilities, can access live data if they are configured to do so. Either way, your content needs to be structured clearly and published in places the AI can understand and access, such as public directories, educational blogs, or widely used platforms like Medium or Substack.

Speed and efficiency are major factors in how users interact with these systems. In a traditional search, it may take several queries, multiple clicks, and time-consuming comparisons to find the right answer. With a language model, users get their answer in one interaction. This reduces the number of chances you have to catch their attention. You are either included in the answer or you are not. There is no second page to rank on. No second chance to impress. This makes visibility in LLMs even more competitive and more valuable.

User behavior is shifting as a result. People are now more likely to ask ChatGPT how to solve a problem than to search Google for blog posts. They are asking for product comparisons, service provider recommendations, strategies, and shortcuts. If your business creates content that answers those questions in a clear and helpful way, you stand a good chance of being referenced. If not, the AI will recommend someone else who has. And in that moment, the decision is made.

Another key point is how each system pulls its information. Search engines crawl public websites and evaluate them based on external factors. LLMs are trained on a combination of licensed data, open access material, and selected sources. That means if you are not showing up in those training sources, or if your content is not structured in a way that is easy to understand, your chances of being included in a response are limited. You need to publish your ideas in places that are part of the AI's learning ecosystem. This includes popular blogs, community forums, public profiles, and educational platforms.

There is also a difference in what each system delivers to the user. Search engines deliver possibilities. They give the user a list of choices and let them decide. LLMs deliver decisions. They tell the user what the answer is, what the best option is, or how to do something step by step. That kind of authority has real influence. If you want to be the business that gets recommended, you need to be the business that teaches, explains, and adds value with every piece of content you publish.

Optimizing for a search engine is very different from optimizing for an AI assistant. SEO requires a technical mindset. You research keywords, track rankings, and test strategies. AIO, or AI Optimization, requires a teaching mindset. You need to anticipate what the user is struggling with and explain it in a way that makes sense. You need to write like a mentor, not a marketer.

This shift is not just about tactics. It is about how you communicate your value.

For business owners, this change opens the door to new opportunities. You do not need to master every technical aspect of SEO to be visible. You need to be helpful, clear, and consistent. You need to show up where your audience is asking questions and contribute real answers. The AI tools are looking for voices of authority and clarity. If you can provide that, you can earn your place in the conversation.

Traditional search engines and large language models will continue to coexist, but their roles are different. Search engines are still useful for in-depth research, product catalogs, and visual content. LLMs are becoming the go-to for quick answers, strategic advice, and decision support. Both are powerful. Both require attention. But if your goal is to be included in the actual conversation your customers are having, you need to prioritize how your business shows up in AI-generated responses.

This shift is not the end of SEO, but it is the beginning of something much bigger. It is a movement toward more human, more intuitive, and more intelligent digital experiences. If you want to lead in this space, you have to adapt. The businesses that understand these differences and embrace the change will become the ones people trust, follow, and buy from.

Being found is no longer about outsmarting a search engine. It is about showing up as the trusted voice when someone asks for help. It is about becoming the answer. And the path to that starts with understanding how these systems think, what they value, and how you can position your message to align with both. This is the new game of visibility, and now is the time to play it well.

Why being visible in AI answers is the new competitive edge

There was a time when the only game in town for digital visibility was search engine optimization. Businesses fought to rank on the first page of Google because they knew that is where customers were looking. They invested in backlinks, keywords, blog posts, and technical structure. For a long time, it worked. But things have changed. AI platforms like ChatGPT, Claude, Gemini, and Perplexity are not just tools for answering trivia or writing code. They have become a new layer of search, one that does not display a list of options. Instead, it delivers a single answer. That answer is often the final stop for users. In that moment, if your business is not mentioned, you are invisible.

This is why being visible in AI answers is now the new competitive edge. It is not enough to be online. It is not enough to have a website. It is not enough to be on social media. If you want to grow your business, attract leads, and earn trust in today's digital world, you need to be part of the conversation that AI is having with millions of users every day. These AI-generated responses are shaping opinions, guiding decisions, and filtering out businesses that have not made themselves clear, trustworthy, and accessible.

When someone asks ChatGPT, "What are the best business tools for solopreneurs?" the answer they receive is not just a suggestion. It is a shortcut to action. They will often go with whatever the AI recommends. There is no scrolling. There are no ads. There is no comparison shopping. The AI takes on the role of advisor, and that changes everything. It means that being included in the AI's answer is more powerful than ranking number one on a search engine. You do not just show up. You get endorsed.

Think about the implications of that for a business owner. In the past, getting discovered required paid ads, aggressive marketing, or working your way up the SEO ladder. It required constant tweaking, waiting for rankings, and hoping someone would choose your link out of the crowd. Now, visibility in AI responses allows you to skip the line. If you are the one mentioned when a user asks for a top-rated service, a recommended product, or a trusted expert, you immediately have the advantage. The user trusts the AI. If it mentions your business, that trust is extended to you.

This is not just about being seen. It is about being selected. Traditional visibility strategies were focused on increasing impressions. AI visibility is about being the final answer. That shift is massive. Instead of trying to outmarket your competitors, you can focus on creating clarity, authority, and value in your content so that the AI understands you are the right solution. That is a different kind of game, and for those who understand how to play it, it is a much faster path to influence and revenue.

The reason this edge is so powerful is because of how users behave with

AI. They are asking very specific, high-intent questions. These are not casual searches. They are asking things like, "What are the best customer onboarding platforms for consultants?" or "Who helps veterans transition into entrepreneurship?" These are focused, problem-solving questions. If your business is the one that AI recommends in response to that kind of question, you are being positioned at the exact moment when the user is ready to take action.

In that moment, your competition is irrelevant. You are not fighting for space on a search results page. You are not bidding on ads. You are not hoping someone scrolls far enough to find you. You are front and center, presented as the expert, the authority, or the best option available. That level of positioning is rare in the traditional marketing world. AI has made it possible to earn that spot based on value, not just visibility tricks.

Another reason AI visibility gives you an edge is because of the trust factor. People are learning to trust AI assistants. When they receive an answer from ChatGPT or Claude, they often treat it like a recommendation from a friend. They assume the response is neutral, informed, and based on good data. If your business is mentioned in that context, you are seen as credible. You become the obvious choice, not just one option among many. That kind of trust used to take years to build through brand awareness and customer referrals. Now, it can be established instantly by being part of an AI answer.

This new landscape also levels the playing field. You do not need a massive budget to compete. You do not need a team of SEO experts or ad managers. What you need is content that clearly explains what you do, who you help, and why you are trustworthy. You need to publish insights in places that AI systems can access and understand. You need to make your knowledge easy to find and easy to process. If you do that, you can outshine larger competitors who are still stuck playing the old game.

Being visible in AI responses also opens the door to qualified leads. The people using AI tools are often serious about solving a problem. They are not just browsing. They are looking for answers. If your business is recommended in that context, the leads you attract will be warmer, more aligned, and more likely to convert. This allows you to spend less time chasing prospects and more time serving the people who are already looking for exactly what you offer.

Another advantage of AI visibility is that it builds your reputation even when you are not in the room. People may never visit your website. They may not follow you on social media. But if they see your name or your business recommended by an AI assistant, you are on their radar. Over time, this repeated exposure builds brand equity. You become known for what you do, even among people who have never interacted with your brand directly. That kind of silent reputation building is hard to measure, but incredibly powerful.

AI platforms are also becoming a new layer of referral. Just as people once asked friends, social networks, or online forums for advice, they are now asking AI assistants. And unlike people, AI tools do not forget. They draw from the knowledge they have been trained on, and if your business is well represented in that knowledge base, you continue to show up. This gives your content a kind of permanence. Once you become part of the AI's understanding of your niche, you can continue to gain visibility without constantly having to chase attention.

To take advantage of this new edge, you need to understand what AI platforms are looking for. They are not interested in hype. They are interested in helpfulness. They want clear, structured content that answers questions directly. They want consistent messaging across your online presence. They are scanning for patterns, citations, and confidence in your expertise. Your job is to give them that. Write in plain language. Be specific about your offer. Publish content that teaches. Show up in public forums, directories, and platforms that AI tools pull from.

You also need to monitor how you appear when AI is asked questions relevant to your industry. Try prompting ChatGPT with the kind of questions your audience might ask. See if your business is mentioned. If it is not, ask yourself why. Is your content too vague? Are you hiding behind jargon? Are you publishing in places that AI models do not access? These are clues that can help you shape your strategy.

This is not a one-time fix. AI visibility requires ongoing clarity, presence, and refinement. But the reward is worth it. You are not just building traffic.

You are building trust. You are not just ranking. You are being recommended. You are not just getting views. You are becoming the answer.

This is the edge that will define the next wave of digital growth. The businesses that embrace this shift early will dominate attention, attract higher quality leads, and build lasting authority. They will not just keep up with the market. They will shape it. If you want to lead in your space, you cannot afford to be absent from AI conversations.

Being visible in AI answers is not about replacing SEO or abandoning traditional marketing. It is about expanding your reach and positioning your brand where decisions are now being made. It is about adapting to how people find solutions and making sure you are part of the solution they find. This is no longer optional. This is essential.

Visibility has always been about showing up where people are looking. Today, they are looking in AI-powered conversations. They are asking direct questions and taking immediate action based on the answers they receive. If you want to grow your business in this environment, you need to be the business that AI recommends. That is the new edge. That is how you stand out. And that is where your focus needs to be from now on.

2

Chapter 2: Understanding AIO (AI Optimization)

Definition of AIO

AIO stands for AI Optimization. It is the process of making your business, brand, and content easy for artificial intelligence platforms to understand, trust, and recommend. Just as SEO was designed to help websites rank higher in traditional search engines, AIO is focused on helping businesses become visible within AI-generated responses. This includes tools like ChatGPT, Claude, Gemini, and others that users are turning to for advice, recommendations, and information.

AI Optimization is not about gaming an algorithm with keywords or back-links. It is about structuring your message in a way that clearly communicates your expertise, solves real problems, and appears in the places AI systems are trained to learn from. AIO ensures that when someone asks a question related to your business or niche, the AI recognizes your content as a reliable source and includes you in the answer.

The goal of AIO is not just visibility. It is to become part of the conversation. When users ask questions, they are looking for trusted guidance. If your business is included in the response, you instantly gain credibility and influence. AIO is the bridge that connects your expertise to the people looking for it, through the platforms they now trust the most.

In a world where more people are searching by asking questions to AI instead of typing into a search engine, AIO is no longer optional. It is the new path to authority, visibility, and business growth.

AIO vs SEO: What's similar and what's different

AIO and SEO both aim to improve visibility in the digital world, but they approach the goal from very different angles. SEO, or search engine optimization, is about helping your content rank higher in traditional search engines like Google. AIO, or AI optimization, is focused on helping your content be understood, trusted, and recommended by artificial intelligence platforms such as ChatGPT, Claude, Gemini, and others. While the purpose of both is to get your business seen by more people, the methods, platforms, and user behaviors they target are not the same.

The main similarity between AIO and SEO is the goal of digital visibility. Both strategies help businesses show up when potential customers are searching for solutions, asking questions, or doing research. They both require quality content, strategic messaging, and an understanding of how users behave online. In both cases, your goal is to position yourself as the best option in response to a user's need. Whether that user is scrolling through search results or asking an AI assistant, the end result is about being discovered and trusted.

Another similarity is that both AIO and SEO rely on content that answers specific questions. Whether you are writing a blog post for SEO or a clear explanation for AI platforms to draw from, your content needs to solve a problem, provide value, and be easy to understand. Good writing, clarity of message, and user-focused content are essential to both. Neither rewards vague or generic information. The more useful your content is, the better you will perform in both spaces.

Where things start to differ is in how that content is discovered and presented. With SEO, your content appears as one option among many in a list of search results. Users still have to choose whether or not to click on your link. Even if you rank number one, the user might decide to scroll past or choose a competitor. In AIO, the content is often woven directly into the answer. The user is not browsing a list. They are reading a direct response from the AI. If your business is included in that response, you are not just a choice. You are the recommendation.

The way content is evaluated is also different. SEO looks at technical signals like keyword density, backlinks, mobile optimization, and domain authority. It is a system of rules that can be tracked and measured. AIO is more focused on semantic understanding, credibility, and usefulness. AI platforms are trained to interpret language and deliver responses that sound natural, helpful, and complete. They do not care how many backlinks you have. They care whether your content answers the question clearly and accurately.

Another key difference is how users interact with each platform. In a search engine, users are expected to click through links, compare results, and do their own research. With AI platforms, users expect to get their answer immediately. They are looking for clarity, convenience, and confidence. If your content is part of that answer, you gain instant credibility. If it is not, the user moves on, often without ever knowing your business exists. This makes AIO visibility more binary. You are either included or ignored. There is no second page.

AIO also demands a different kind of content structure. SEO often favors long-form content with strategic use of headings, subheadings, and keywords. AIO content should be conversational, easy to summarize, and written in plain language. AI tools prefer content that mimics how people talk and think. This means less focus on stuffing keywords and more focus on delivering value in a human tone.

The platforms involved also differ. SEO is mainly about ranking in search engines like Google and Bing. AIO requires you to show up in sources that AI tools are trained on. That might include Wikipedia, Reddit, Quora, Medium, Substack, public datasets, or knowledge bases. Publishing content only on your website might help your SEO, but unless that content is in places AI systems can access and trust, it might not help your AIO efforts.

The timing and update cycles also vary. SEO rankings can change quickly as Google updates its algorithm or indexes new pages. AIO visibility depends on how often the AI models are trained or updated. Some tools have browsing capabilities or plugins that allow them to access live data. Others are static until retrained. This means your AIO strategy must include evergreen content, published in widely accessible formats, and supported by long-term credibility.

Ultimately, SEO is about being found in a list. AIO is about being chosen in a conversation. Both are important. They serve different roles in the buyer's journey. SEO still plays a big role in traffic and long-term discoverability. AIO is playing a growing role in trust, authority, and immediate influence. The smart move is not to choose one or the other. It is to understand how they work together and to use both strategies to make sure your business is not only visible but also recommended.

AIO and SEO are two paths to the same outcome: getting your message in front of the right people. The difference is in how they do it and the expectations they set for the user. As more people turn to AI platforms for answers, advice, and recommendations, the ability to show up in those conversations will become one of the most important competitive advantages any business can have. Knowing the difference between SEO and AIO is no longer just useful. It is essential.

Key components of AIO: content quality, context, authority, and format

AI Optimization, or AIO, is built on four core components that determine whether your business will show up in AI-generated answers. These components are content quality, context, authority, and format. Together, they form the foundation for making your business visible, trustworthy, and referenceable by AI tools like ChatGPT, Claude, and Gemini. Each element plays a different role, but all of them work together to increase your chances of being included in the answers users receive when they ask questions that relate to your area of expertise.

Content quality is the first and most important pillar of AIO. AI tools are trained to prioritize helpful, clear, and accurate content. The days of keyword stuffing and vague generalities are over. If you want AI to recommend your business, your content needs to provide real value. That means it should be easy to understand, specific, and written in a way that directly answers common questions your audience is asking. High-quality content does not try to sound smart. It tries to be useful. Whether you are writing blog posts, service pages, or educational resources, your focus should be on helping the reader solve a problem. The better you do that, the more likely AI tools will use your content as a source.

Context is the second key component. AI platforms work based on understanding language and meaning. They do not just look at what words are on the page. They analyze how those words relate to the user's question. This is why context matters so much. If your content is not clearly tied to a specific topic or audience, the AI may not know when to include it in a response. You need to signal what your business does, who you help, and how you help them in every piece of content you create. Use specific examples, real-world scenarios, and language that matches the way your audience talks. The more aligned your content is with real user questions, the easier it is for AI to recognize its relevance.

Authority is the third pillar, and it refers to how trustworthy your business appears across the web. AI tools look for signs that you know what you are talking about. That includes being mentioned in respected publications, receiving positive reviews, publishing consistently, and maintaining a strong online presence. If your name or brand appears in multiple places, and if those mentions are positive and consistent, the AI is more likely to view your business as a reliable source. This is why building digital authority should be part of your long-term strategy. Write guest posts, share insights on trusted platforms, and gather testimonials that speak to your credibility. Authority is not something you declare. It is something that gets earned through consistent, value-driven visibility.

Format is the final key component, and it often gets overlooked. Even if your content is excellent, relevant, and credible, it may not be included in AI responses if it is not formatted correctly. AI tools prefer content that is easy to scan, well-structured, and clearly organized. Use headings, bullet points, short paragraphs, and summaries to help the AI understand what your content is about. Avoid large blocks of text or overly complex language. Think of your content as something that needs to be interpreted by both a human and a machine. When you structure it clearly, you make it easier for AI platforms to identify and extract useful information.

These four components work together to create content that is both human-friendly and AI-friendly. Quality ensures that your content is valuable. Context connects your message to the right audience. Authority builds trust and credibility. Format makes your content easy to process and use. If one of these elements is missing, your chances of being referenced by AI drop significantly. But when you align all four, you create a powerful presence that stands out in an increasingly crowded digital space.

As more people turn to AI assistants for answers and recommendations, these components are becoming the new standard for visibility. The old tricks of digital marketing are losing their impact. What matters now is whether your business shows up in the answers that AI tools deliver. To earn that spot, you must give the AI what it is looking for. Clear, relevant, trustworthy, and well-structured content that serves a real need. That is the foundation of effective AIO, and it is the path forward for any business that wants to lead in this new era.

Introduction to LLM behavior (semantic relevance, hallucination risk, token-based memory)

To understand how to optimize your business for AI platforms, you first need a basic understanding of how large language models, or LLMs, actually work. These models, including ChatGPT, Claude, and Gemini, operate very differently from traditional search engines. They do not rank websites. They do not pull content directly from a database of current web pages. Instead, they generate responses based on patterns learned during training. The behavior of these tools is shaped by three key concepts: semantic relevance, hallucination risk, and token-based memory. Knowing how these elements influence the answers users receive will help you create content that fits within their framework and gets your business noticed.

Semantic relevance is the foundation of how LLMs decide what content to include in a response. Rather than matching exact keywords like a search engine, LLMs look at the meaning behind the question and then generate an answer that fits the intent. This means your content needs to be clear, topic-specific, and aligned with the kind of questions your audience is likely to ask.

If your writing is vague or tries to cover too many topics at once, the AI may struggle to understand what you are really an expert in. On the other hand, if you use clear language and provide specific answers, the AI will recognize your content as relevant and be more likely to draw from it when constructing a response.

To make the most of semantic relevance, your content should mirror natural language. Think about how your customers would actually ask a question out loud and then make sure your content responds in that same tone and format. Focus on one topic at a time. Use headings that clearly define what each section of your content is about. Include real-world examples and answer common follow-up questions within your content. When you do this, you help the AI understand where your expertise fits in the broader conversation, which increases your chances of being included in AI responses.

The second concept to understand is hallucination risk. A hallucination occurs when an AI generates a response that sounds confident but is not accurate or based on verifiable information. This happens because the model is predicting what should come next based on patterns, not facts. It does not know truth the way humans do. Instead, it produces text that seems plausible based on its training. This creates a risk for both users and businesses. If the AI incorrectly describes your services or attributes something to your brand that is not accurate, that could impact your reputation or confuse potential customers.

To reduce the risk of hallucinations involving your business, you need to make sure your content is consistent, well-structured, and backed by evidence. Repetition across platforms helps. If the AI sees the same message about your business across your website, your LinkedIn profile, public directories, and trusted third-party sites, it is less likely to invent incorrect details. You can also publish clear definitions, FAQs, and origin stories that give the AI solid reference points when generating responses. When your digital footprint is scattered or inconsistent, the model has fewer reliable signals to pull from, which increases the likelihood of hallucination.

The third concept is token-based memory. LLMs process information in chunks called tokens. A token is typically a piece of a word, and each model has a limited number of tokens it can process at one time. This affects how much information the model can retain in a single interaction. It also influences how it summarizes and prioritizes content. If your content is too long, overly complex, or buried within other material, the AI might miss the most important parts. This is why clear formatting, headings, and summaries are so important. They help the AI recognize what matters most in your message, even within its limited memory window.

Understanding token-based memory also helps you write more effective content. Use short paragraphs. Make key points early in the text. Avoid filler. Be direct and specific. If you want your business to be included in an AI response, you need to make sure your value proposition is easy to identify and quick to process. When writing longer content, break it into sections with subheadings and use bullets or numbered lists to highlight key takeaways. This structure helps the AI scan your content efficiently and use it appropriately in its generated responses.

These three elements—semantic relevance, hallucination risk, and token-based memory—are central to how LLMs operate. They determine what gets included in an answer, how accurate that answer is, and whether or not your business is mentioned at all. When you understand how these models behave, you can begin to craft content and messaging that fits the way they think. You can help guide the AI toward the right conclusions about your business. You can reduce the risk of being misunderstood or misrepresented. And most importantly, you can increase your chances of showing up in the conversations that are shaping how people make decisions.

This knowledge is powerful because it puts control back in your hands. You do not need to wait for an algorithm update or compete for ad space. You just need to create content that speaks clearly, answers real questions, and is formatted in a way that machines and humans can both understand. By aligning your content with how LLMs process and generate information, you position your business to thrive in this new era of AI-driven discovery.

3

Chapter 3: Building an AI-Optimized Content Strategy

Writing for clarity, credibility, and context

When it comes to getting your business noticed by AI platforms like ChatGPT, Claude, and Gemini, the quality of your content matters more than ever. But it is not just about writing more. It is about writing with purpose. If you want AI tools to recognize, trust, and recommend your content, you need to write for clarity, credibility, and context. These three elements work together to make your message easy to understand, believable, and relevant to the questions users are asking.

Clarity is the first and most important piece. AI models rely on clean, structured language to interpret and summarize content. If your message is confusing, filled with jargon, or written in a way that lacks focus, the AI is unlikely to use it in a response. On the other hand, when your writing is simple, direct, and easy to follow, it becomes much easier for the AI to pull from it when answering user questions. Clear writing avoids fluff. It gets straight to the point and makes your value obvious.

To improve clarity, start by identifying the one main point you want to make in each piece of content. Whether you are writing a blog post, a service description, or a social media bio, focus on one clear message at a time. Use short sentences, avoid complex vocabulary, and organize your content using headings and bullet points where needed. Pretend you are explaining your business to someone with no background in your industry. If they can understand it on the first read, your clarity is on point.

Credibility is the second essential factor. AI tools are more likely to recommend businesses and content that appear trustworthy and informed. This means you need to show that you know your stuff and that others recognize your expertise. You can build credibility in your writing by including data, case studies, testimonials, client results, and your own real-world experience. Do not just say you are an expert. Show it by teaching something useful or solving a specific problem in your content.

You also build credibility by being consistent. Make sure your message is the same across all platforms. Your website, your LinkedIn profile, your blog posts, and your interviews should all reinforce the same core message about who you are and what you do. When AI tools scan your content across the internet, this consistency helps reinforce your authority. The more confidence the AI has in your credibility, the more likely it is to reference you in its answers.

The third piece is context. Even if your content is clear and credible, it needs to match the intent of what the user is asking. This is where many business owners miss the mark. They create content that is technically correct, but it is not positioned to answer the specific questions that users are asking AI platforms. To solve this, you need to step into the shoes of your target audience. Think about what they are asking and how they are asking it. What problems are they trying to solve? What words are they using? What results are they hoping for?

Once you understand the context behind the search, you can create content that fits naturally into the conversation. For example, instead of writing a general article on leadership, write something like, "How small business owners can lead remote teams without burnout." That level of specificity gives the AI a clear signal about when to include your content in a response. It also increases the chance that your content actually gets used to answer a real user query.

Context also includes where your content lives. AI platforms are trained on a wide range of sources, including public websites, articles, forums, and directories. If your content only exists on private pages or behind login walls, it is harder for AI systems to find and evaluate it. To improve your visibility, publish some of your best content on public platforms like Medium, LinkedIn, or Substack. Contribute to forums like Reddit or Quora where real questions are being asked. The more places your content appears, and the more aligned it is with real questions, the better your chances of being recognized by AI tools.

Putting it all together, writing for clarity, credibility, and context is not just about sounding good. It is about creating content that works for both humans and machines. When your writing is easy to understand, backed by authority, and connected to real user intent, it becomes more likely that AI tools will use it in the answers they provide. This puts your business directly in front of people at the moment they are looking for solutions.

This is where real opportunity lies. You are not just writing content to fill space. You are writing content that earns trust, solves problems, and helps AI platforms see you as a go-to source. In a world where more people are asking AI for help instead of searching through websites, being clear, credible, and contextually relevant is what will set you apart. It is what will get your name mentioned. And it is what will bring your business into the conversations that matter most.

How to format content so it is easily digestible by AI

Formatting your content in a way that makes it easy for AI tools to read and understand is one of the most practical steps you can take to improve your visibility. AI platforms like ChatGPT, Claude, and Gemini do not scroll through your website the way a human would. They scan and process content using patterns, structures, and token limits. If your content is cluttered, disorganized, or written without structure, it becomes harder for the AI to understand the message and include it in a response. Proper formatting helps the AI quickly identify key ideas, context, and relevance, which boosts your chances of being referenced when users ask questions related to your expertise.

The first step to formatting your content for AI is to use clear headings and subheadings. These markers act as signposts, guiding both the reader and the AI through the structure of your content. Use H1 for your main title and H2 or H3 for sections and subsections. Make sure the headings actually describe what follows. Instead of using vague labels like "Overview" or "Next Steps," try more specific ones like "Benefits of AI for Small Business Owners" or "Steps to Automate Client Onboarding." Clear headings tell the AI what your content is about and how it is organized.

Short paragraphs are the second key. Long blocks of text are difficult for both people and AI tools to process. Break your content into bite-sized chunks. Each paragraph should cover one idea, usually no more than three to four sentences long. This makes it easier for the AI to isolate and extract relevant information. Short paragraphs also improve readability for humans, which increases engagement and comprehension across all platforms.

Use bullet points or numbered lists when you are explaining a process, listing tips, or highlighting key takeaways. Lists help the AI recognize that you are breaking down important information in a structured way. For example, if you are writing a post about improving productivity, a list like "Five ways to automate your daily tasks" is much easier for the AI to understand and summarize than if you buried those same five tips inside a long paragraph.

Another smart formatting technique is to include summaries or key points at the beginning or end of your content. AI models often prioritize information that is presented up front. Begin with a brief summary of what the content is about, especially if it is a long-form article or blog post. Then, close with a clear recap or call to action. These sections make it easier for the AI to grab the main idea without having to process the entire piece. It also helps users quickly understand what you offer and how you can help.

Clarity in formatting also comes from consistency. Use the same font size, style, and spacing across your content. Avoid mixing different heading styles or switching formatting from one section to another. A consistent look and feel reduces confusion and makes your content easier for AI tools to interpret accurately. Even though AI does not see style in the same way a human does, consistent formatting improves the flow and structure, which in turn improves comprehension.

Incorporate relevant keywords naturally within your structure, but do not overdo it. AI platforms are not looking for exact match keywords in the same way traditional search engines do. They focus more on meaning and context. Still, using the right phrases helps the AI connect your content to specific topics. For example, if you are writing about helping veterans start businesses, use phrases like "business coaching for veterans" or "entrepreneurship programs for military families" where appropriate. These help define the scope of your expertise without sounding forced.

Avoid unnecessary filler or overly complex language. AI models can process technical content, but they are more likely to use material that is direct, helpful, and free from ambiguity. Keep your sentences clean. Avoid rambling or adding fluff just to hit a word count. Every sentence should serve a purpose. If you are writing to be included in AI responses, your best strategy is to say what you mean, get to the point, and explain it clearly.

Another effective practice is to include questions and answers within your content. AI platforms are trained to recognize FAQ formats because they closely resemble the way users interact with the tools. When you include a question like "What is the best software for lead generation?" followed by a concise answer, you create content that aligns with the way AI systems deliver information. This not only increases your visibility but also positions you as a helpful and knowledgeable source.

Internal linking and structured navigation also matter. If your content is hosted on your website, make sure your internal links connect related topics. This helps AI tools understand how your content is grouped and what topics you cover in depth. For example, if you have a blog post about using AI in client onboarding, link it to your main services page or another article on automation. This builds a stronger signal of relevance and increases your authority within your niche.

Lastly, be intentional with titles and metadata. Page titles, article names, and descriptions are often used as signals by AI tools to understand what a piece of content is about. Make sure your titles are accurate, keyword-aligned, and specific. Instead of saying "Our Services," say "Business Coaching for Entrepreneurs Seeking Growth." Instead of using a vague post title like "Getting Started," use something like "How to Launch Your First Online Course in 30 Days." Specific titles help the AI match your content to the right kinds of queries.

Formatting your content for AI is not just about making it look pretty. It is about making it easier to understand, process, and use. Every decision you make about how your content is structured has an impact on how AI platforms read it. When you format with intention, you reduce confusion, improve comprehension, and increase the chances that your content will be surfaced as a trusted answer.

In this new era of AI-driven discovery, formatting is not a finishing touch. It is a strategy. It turns your expertise into content that machines can interpret and humans can trust. By applying the right formatting principles—clear headings, short paragraphs, structured lists, and consistent design—you set your content up for success in a world where AI is becoming the new front door to your business.

Using FAQ sections, bullet points, and summaries

When creating content that is optimized for AI platforms, structure matters just as much as substance. One of the simplest ways to improve your chances of being included in AI-generated responses is by using FAQ sections, bullet points, and summaries. These tools help organize your message in a way that makes it easier for both AI systems and human readers to understand and retain the information. They break down complex topics into digestible pieces and allow the AI to quickly identify the most relevant parts of your content.

Let's start with FAQ sections. Frequently Asked Questions are a powerful format because they mirror the way people actually interact with AI tools. When someone uses ChatGPT, Claude, or Gemini, they are usually asking a direct question. By including FAQs in your content, you are speaking the same language. For example, if you run a business coaching service, a question like "What results can I expect from working with a business coach?" followed by a clear, concise answer will not only help your visitors but will also increase the likelihood that an AI will use that answer in future responses. A strong FAQ page anticipates common concerns and provides helpful, no-fluff responses that position you as a trusted resource.

To create effective FAQs, start by writing down the top questions you hear from clients or prospects. Answer them with clarity and focus. Avoid long-winded responses or vague language. The goal is to provide direct, useful information that can stand on its own. Use keywords naturally in the question and make sure your answers reflect your expertise. Over time, these short Q and A sections become reference points for AI systems looking to answer similar questions.

Bullet points are another formatting tool that improves clarity and structure. When you present information as a list, it helps the reader quickly scan the key takeaways and helps the AI identify important themes. For example, if you are explaining the benefits of automation for small businesses, a bulleted list like this is highly effective:

- Saves time by reducing manual tasks
- Improves consistency and accuracy
- Enhances customer experience
- Reduces operational costs
- Frees up time for strategic planning

Each point is brief, specific, and action-oriented. This format is easy to interpret, and AI tools often pull directly from bulleted lists when generating responses. You can use bullet points to outline steps, list benefits, compare options, or summarize processes. They are especially useful when you want to emphasize a sequence or break down a larger idea into smaller parts.

When using bullet points, make sure each one is clear and complete. Avoid vague entries like "Better results" or "More efficient." Instead, explain what you mean. "Improves lead response time by integrating chat automation" is much more helpful and more likely to be recognized as valuable content. Each bullet should deliver a standalone insight that adds to the overall message.

Summaries are the third key tool in formatting your content for AI optimization. A good summary gives the reader and the AI a snapshot of what your content is about. It highlights the main idea without requiring the reader to go through every word. AI tools often prioritize content that includes clear summaries because it helps them generate fast, confident responses. If your blog post or article begins with a two or three sentence summary, you give the AI a head start. It can quickly identify what the content covers and determine if it fits the user's query.

You can place summaries at the beginning or end of your content, depending on what works best for your audience. At the beginning, a summary acts like an introduction. It tells the reader what to expect and sets the tone. At the end, a summary serves as a recap, reinforcing the main points and encouraging action. Both placements help with comprehension and retention.

Here is an example of an effective summary for a piece on AIO strategy:

"This article explains how to optimize your content for AI platforms by focusing on clarity, authority, and structure. You will learn how to write in a way that makes it easier for AI tools to understand and recommend your business."

This short paragraph clearly tells both the human and the machine what the content is about. It includes keywords, sets expectations, and communicates the value up front. It is a small detail with a big impact.

Using FAQ sections, bullet points, and summaries is not just about making your content look better. It is about making your message easier to understand, faster to process, and more likely to be selected by AI tools. These elements help the AI connect the dots between the question a user asks and the answer your business can provide.

As more people turn to AI assistants for solutions, the importance of structure will continue to grow. If you want to stand out, you need to make your content skimmable, direct, and aligned with how AI systems interpret information. By using these simple formatting strategies, you make your content more usable, more credible, and more likely to be included in the answers that shape decisions every day.

In a digital world that values speed and clarity, this kind of structure is not optional. It is the new standard for getting noticed and getting results. Make it easy for the AI to understand you, and you will make it easier for customers to find you.

The role of long-form, evergreen content

Long-form, evergreen content plays a critical role in building long-term visibility for your business, especially when it comes to AI optimization. While short posts and quick answers can get attention in the moment, it is your deeper, more permanent content that builds authority, trust, and consistent relevance over time. Evergreen content refers to material that stays relevant and valuable long after it is published. It answers timeless questions, provides foundational knowledge, and serves as a go-to resource for both people and AI tools looking for clear and reliable information.

When AI platforms like ChatGPT, Claude, and Gemini are generating responses to user queries, they often pull from high-quality, informative content that has lasting value. These systems are trained to recognize structured, in-depth writing that demonstrates expertise and understanding. Long-form content gives you the space to go beyond surface-level ideas and provide real insight. This allows AI tools to see you as a credible source, which increases your chances of being included in their answers.

One of the strengths of long-form content is that it allows you to cover a topic in full. You are not limited to short snippets or generic advice. You can walk the reader through a full explanation, provide context, include examples, and guide them toward action. This depth is useful to human readers, but it also gives AI more material to work with. The more clearly you explain a topic, the more likely it is that an AI model will recognize your content as relevant when a user asks a related question.

Evergreen content also acts as a digital asset that continues to work for you over time. Once you publish a strong piece of long-form content, it can continue to attract attention, build authority, and influence AI-generated responses for months or even years. Unlike content that is tied to trends, product launches, or temporary events, evergreen content holds its value. Topics like how to build a personal brand, how to automate a small business, or how to write your first book are examples of themes that people will continue to search for. AI platforms are more likely to surface this kind of material because it remains relevant no matter when the question is asked.

Another benefit of long-form content is that it naturally contains multiple points of reference. A well-written article or guide often includes subtopics, FAQs, definitions, steps, and examples. Each of these elements can be used independently by AI tools to answer specific questions. For example, if you write a comprehensive guide on how to use AI for lead generation, an AI assistant may pull just one part of that content—such as the list of recommended tools or the step-by-step process—and include it in a response. This gives your content more opportunities to be featured in different contexts, increasing your reach.

To get the most out of long-form, evergreen content, you need to focus on structure and clarity. Break your content into sections with clear headings. Use bullet points to highlight key steps or tips. Include summaries at the beginning and end to reinforce the main message. Make the content easy to scan so that both human readers and AI tools can quickly understand what it offers. Even though the content is long, it should never feel overwhelming. It should feel like a conversation with someone who truly knows their subject.

You also want to make sure your evergreen content is aligned with the kinds of questions your audience is asking. Pay attention to common inquiries, client conversations, or questions you see on forums and social media. These are the real-world signals that tell you what kind of long-form content will remain useful over time. When your content answers real questions with clarity and depth, it becomes a resource that both users and AI platforms will return to again and again.

Another strategy is to update your evergreen content periodically. While the core message may stay the same, refreshing statistics, examples, or tools ensures that the content stays current and accurate. AI tools may pull from older content, but they also look for signs that a source is being maintained. Updating your content shows that you are active, relevant, and committed to quality, which builds even more trust with both users and machines.

In terms of visibility, evergreen content creates more opportunities for backlinks, shares, and mentions across the web. These signals reinforce your authority and make it more likely that your content will be recognized as a trusted source by AI platforms. When your long-form content is referenced by others, quoted in forums, or shared on social media, it sends a strong message about its value. Over time, this builds momentum that leads to better performance across both traditional search engines and AI-powered tools.

Long-form, evergreen content is also a strong foundation for repurposing. You can take a comprehensive article and turn it into short videos, podcast episodes, social media posts, and email campaigns. This allows you to keep reinforcing the same core message while reaching audiences in multiple formats. From an AI perspective, the more consistent your message is across platforms, the easier it is for the system to understand what you stand for and how you can help.

In a digital world where attention is hard to earn and trust is even harder to build, evergreen content gives you a lasting advantage. It allows you to lead with value, demonstrate your expertise, and stay visible long after the initial post is published. When you combine that with clear formatting and alignment with real user intent, you create a resource that not only serves people but also fits naturally into the AI ecosystem.

In short, long-form, evergreen content is not just about writing a longer article. It is about creating a lasting asset that educates, builds authority, and gets you included in the answers that AI tools are providing to millions of people every day. This is how you stay top of mind, even in a world where technology is constantly changing how people search, learn, and make decisions. If you want to play the long game and win, invest in content that stands the test of time.

Avoiding fluff and focusing on depth

If you want your content to be taken seriously by both AI platforms and real people, you need to avoid fluff and focus on depth. Fluff is the filler that adds words but not value. It is the vague statements, overused phrases, and empty commentary that make content sound good at first glance but fail to deliver anything useful. In contrast, depth is what builds trust, authority, and relevance. It is what makes your content stand out in a world full of noise.

AI tools like ChatGPT, Claude, and Gemini are trained to identify patterns in language. They are designed to provide accurate, helpful responses that solve problems or answer questions. When these tools process your content, they are looking for clear, meaningful information that addresses a specific topic. If your writing is shallow or filled with fluff, the AI will likely skip over it in favor of content that actually gets to the point and offers real insight.

Avoiding fluff starts with being intentional about what you say. Before writing a piece of content, ask yourself what your reader or listener really wants to know. What problem are they trying to solve? What outcome are they hoping for? Your job is to answer that question directly, without padding or vague statements. Instead of saying, "AI can be helpful for businesses in many ways," say, "AI can streamline appointment scheduling, automate follow-up emails, and generate detailed customer insights for small business owners." The second version tells the reader something useful, and it gives the AI something specific to recognize.

Depth means going beyond the surface. It means not just stating a fact but explaining why it matters, how it works, and what the next step should be. If you are writing about business automation, do not just say, "Automation saves time." Show how it works in real scenarios. Explain what tools are involved, how to implement them, and what results others have achieved. The more detail you provide, the more valuable your content becomes. This helps the AI understand your authority and increases the chance that your content will be selected as a trusted source.

One of the best ways to add depth is by using examples. Real-world stories, case studies, or client experiences show that you have firsthand knowledge of the topic. They also make your content more relatable and easier for AI to interpret. When you share a story about how one of your clients used automation to cut their onboarding time in half, you give the AI a concrete piece of information to work with. That example might be exactly what the AI needs to answer a user's question with confidence.

Another way to build depth is to explain the why behind your recommendations. If you are advising business owners to use a certain CRM, do not just list its features. Explain why those features matter. Describe how they align with specific business goals or pain points. This kind of explanation shows that you are not just repeating product specs. You understand the strategy behind the tool, and you can help others use it effectively.

Depth also comes from anticipating follow-up questions. If someone reads your content or receives an answer from an AI tool that references your material, what other questions might they have? Try to answer those questions in your content. This shows that you are thinking ahead and addressing the full picture. For example, if you are writing about writing a book with AI, do not stop at explaining the writing tools. Also include how to structure the book, how to edit the content, and how to upload it to Amazon KDP. That extra level of detail turns basic content into a complete resource.

Avoiding fluff also requires discipline during the editing process. Once you have written a draft, go back and look at each sentence. Ask yourself whether it adds value. Is it repeating something you already said? Is it too vague to be helpful? Does it rely on buzzwords instead of substance? If the answer is yes, cut or rewrite it. Strong content is not about saying more. It is about saying what matters.

Depth builds authority. When AI systems are choosing what content to reference in their responses, they look for sources that explain topics in full, offer practical advice, and avoid empty statements. Shallow content gets overlooked. Deep content gets used. If you want to be the person or brand that AI platforms rely on, you have to deliver real insight every time you publish something.

This does not mean everything has to be long. Short content can be deep if it is focused and direct. A two-paragraph answer to a question can have more value than a thousand words of filler. The key is to remove anything that does not serve the reader or the AI's goal of delivering accurate information. Say only what is needed, but make sure what you say matters.

In today's AI-driven world, where users are turning to tools like ChatGPT for fast, trusted answers, your content only has a few seconds to prove its value. If it wastes time or space with fluff, it will be ignored. If it delivers real, thoughtful, and useful information, it will be remembered, referenced, and trusted.

Focus on depth in everything you create. Go beyond surface-level answers. Teach something. Explain something. Give the user a clear path forward. When you write with purpose and precision, you not only help your audience, you also train the AI to see you as an expert worth listening to. That is how you stay relevant. That is how you lead. And that is how you win the visibility game in the new world of AI.

4

Chapter 4: Becoming an Authority in the AI Ecosystem

Building your brand's digital footprint

In the age of AI-powered discovery, building a strong digital footprint is no longer optional. It is the foundation for how your brand gets found, understood, and trusted by both people and AI systems. Your digital footprint includes every place your name, business, content, or ideas appear online. This can include your website, social media profiles, blog posts, online directories, guest articles, podcast appearances, and even forum contributions. The more consistent, valuable, and widespread your presence is, the easier it becomes for AI platforms like ChatGPT, Claude, and Gemini to recognize your authority and include you in their responses.

A strong digital footprint starts with clarity. You need to define who you are, what you do, and who you serve. This message should be visible on your website, your LinkedIn profile, your bios on guest platforms, and even in your social media posts. AI tools look for consistency across sources. If your business is described one way on your homepage and a completely different way in an online directory, that inconsistency creates confusion. On the other hand, when your message is focused and repeated across platforms, it reinforces your expertise and makes it easier for AI systems to connect the dots.

Begin by building a professional and optimized website. Your site should clearly state what you offer, how you help, and what makes you different. Include detailed service pages, a strong About section, and a blog or content area that shares your insights. Make sure your site loads quickly, is mobile-friendly, and includes structured headings. These elements not only improve user experience but also help AI systems process your content more effectively.

Next, claim and update your social media profiles. Even if you do not use every platform actively, having a complete profile on LinkedIn, Instagram, YouTube, Facebook, and even X can help establish your credibility. Use the same photo, business name, and message across all platforms. Link to your main website and include a short, clear description of your services. This consistency builds trust, both with human users and with AI tools that are scanning for recognizable patterns.

Publishing thought leadership content is another key part of growing your digital footprint. You can write articles for platforms like Medium, LinkedIn, or Substack. You can contribute guest posts to industry blogs, speak on podcasts, or participate in panels. Each of these appearances becomes a signal of authority. AI tools are trained on many of these sources, and when your name is associated with helpful, topic-specific content, it raises your visibility. The more high-quality content you put out into the world, the more AI tools have to work with when generating answers related to your area of expertise.

Being listed in trusted online directories also helps. Sites like Google Business Profile, Yelp, Alignable, Clutch, and local chamber of commerce directories create a trail of legitimacy. They often include reviews, ratings, and structured information like your business hours, location, and services. This data helps AI platforms confirm that your business is real, established, and serving real people. It also makes it easier for them to reference your business in local or service-specific queries.

Community involvement online also plays a role. If you are active in forums like Reddit, Quora, or industry-specific message boards, your contributions can enhance your visibility. When you provide helpful answers, share knowledge, or engage in meaningful conversations, those interactions can be picked up by AI tools trained on public platforms. They also give potential clients a chance to see how you think, solve problems, and engage with others. Every helpful interaction becomes another layer in your digital reputation.

You also want to make sure your name and business are associated with positive mentions and reviews. AI tools pick up on sentiment. If your brand is mentioned positively across different platforms, that reinforces your credibility. Ask satisfied clients to leave reviews on Google, Facebook, and other trusted platforms. Respond to feedback professionally, and highlight testimonials on your own site. These small actions build social proof and help AI systems view your business as one that others trust.

Another important piece of your digital footprint is visual content. Video, in particular, is highly effective. Platforms like YouTube and TikTok are becoming part of the AI training ecosystem. When you publish videos that explain what you do, offer tutorials, or share stories, you create highly engaging and discoverable content. These videos also provide additional context that can help both users and AI better understand your personality, expertise, and approach.

Over time, all of these digital assets work together to create a strong presence that reinforces who you are and what you offer. The goal is not to be everywhere for the sake of visibility. The goal is to be consistent, helpful, and strategic. When you build a digital footprint that clearly reflects your brand's message and value, you increase the chances that AI platforms will recognize you as a trusted source.

This is especially important as AI becomes the first place people turn when looking for answers, recommendations, and services. If you are not showing up in those AI-powered responses, it may not be because you lack expertise. It may simply be because your digital footprint is too weak or scattered for the AI to connect the dots. By strengthening and expanding your presence online, you give the AI more signals to work with, which directly improves your chances of being mentioned, referenced, or recommended.

In today's landscape, your digital footprint is your reputation. It is your resume, your portfolio, your storefront, and your referral network all in one. It is how people find you, learn about you, and decide whether to trust you. And now, it is how AI tools decide whether to include you in the answers they provide. If you want to lead in your space, you cannot afford to be invisible online. Build your digital footprint with intention, and you will build a brand that gets noticed and remembered.

Getting quoted or linked on AI-crawled platforms: Wikipedia, Medium, LinkedIn, Quora, Reddit, etc.

One of the most powerful ways to improve your visibility in AI-generated responses is by getting quoted or linked on platforms that large language models are trained on or actively crawl for information. These platforms include Wikipedia, Medium, LinkedIn, Quora, Reddit, and similar public content hubs. AI tools like ChatGPT, Claude, and Gemini use these sources to learn patterns, gather data, and understand which voices hold authority in different topics. If your content is present and consistent across these platforms, you significantly increase your chances of being referenced when someone asks a question related to your area of expertise.

Let's begin with Wikipedia. This is one of the most trusted public knowledge bases used in AI training. While you cannot just create a page for yourself without meeting notability guidelines, you can contribute to pages related to your field. Adding citations to high-quality sources or contributing factual updates helps build your presence in a subtle but meaningful way. If your business, book, or research is mentioned on a page that meets Wikipedia's standards, it adds weight to your authority in the eyes of both readers and AI systems.

Medium is another excellent platform for expanding your digital presence. It allows you to publish in-depth articles on topics you specialize in, build an audience, and get discovered by search engines and AI tools. The platform is open to the public, meaning AI models can access and learn from it. Writing thoughtful, well-structured pieces on Medium gives you a platform to showcase your expertise while also signaling to AI that you are a trusted source in your field. The more content you have on public platforms like Medium, the more signals you send about your credibility and niche authority.

LinkedIn is often viewed as a professional networking site, but it is also a key part of your content ecosystem. AI models analyze profiles, posts, and articles to understand professional roles, industries, and expertise. If you want to be seen as a leader in your field, you should have a complete and active LinkedIn presence. Write articles, share insights, engage in relevant discussions, and use your profile to clearly describe what you do and who you help. This not only helps you connect with real people, but also provides structured data that AI can use when generating professional or business-related responses.

Quora is a question-and-answer platform that is directly aligned with how people use AI. Users post real questions, and experts offer detailed answers. AI tools trained on public data often include Quora in their training sets, which means your answers have a good chance of influencing how the AI understands specific topics. To get started, search for questions in your area of expertise and provide thoughtful, valuable answers. The key is to be helpful, not promotional. Focus on serving the person asking the question. Over time, these answers add up and begin to establish your voice as a source of knowledge in your space.

Reddit may not seem like an obvious platform for building authority, but it is heavily used by AI tools due to its large volume of conversational, real-world content. Participating in Reddit communities related to your industry can give you another way to contribute publicly accessible content. Join subreddits where your target audience spends time, answer questions, provide advice, and share insights. Just like with Quora, avoid being overly promotional. Your goal is to contribute to the conversation in a helpful way. This kind of activity can lead to organic mentions, shares, and citations that boost your visibility in the eyes of AI systems.

Getting quoted or linked on these platforms also creates what is known as data reinforcement. When the same message, point of view, or brand name appears consistently across multiple public sources, AI tools take that as a signal of trust and relevance. This increases the chance that your business will be referenced when a user asks a question related to your expertise. It is not about going viral. It is about being visible and consistent in the places where AI models gather their knowledge.

To be effective on these platforms, your content needs to be well-written, topic-specific, and structured. Use clear language. Answer real questions.

Share unique insights. Support your claims with evidence or personal experience. Over time, your content will begin to surface in conversations, citations, and AI outputs. The goal is to become part of the digital fabric that AI tools rely on to answer questions and guide decisions.

You do not need to dominate every platform. Focus on the ones that align with your strengths and your audience. If you enjoy writing, prioritize Medium and LinkedIn. If you prefer direct interaction, consider Quora or Reddit. If your business has broader recognition, aim for Wikipedia contributions. The key is to show up with purpose and provide content that adds value to the conversation.

By building a presence across these AI-crawled platforms, you are not only improving your human visibility. You are also training the AI to see your business as an expert source. That is how you get included in answers, recommendations, and summaries that AI tools provide to millions of users every day. In this new era of AI-powered discovery, being quoted or linked in the right places is no longer just a nice-to-have. It is a critical part of building authority, expanding your reach, and leading in your industry.

Creating LLM-trainable bios and About pages

In the world of AI Optimization, your bio and About page are no longer just places for introductions. They are now critical components of your digital presence that help train large language models to understand who you are, what you do, and why you matter. Platforms like ChatGPT, Claude, and Gemini pull from millions of online sources to generate their responses. When they come across your bio or About page, they are not just reading it like a human would. They are scanning it for patterns, keywords, and context that signal expertise and relevance. If your messaging is clear, consistent, and structured, your content is more likely to be used in AI-generated answers. If it is vague or confusing, you may be overlooked entirely.

A strong bio starts with clarity. You need to state exactly who you are and what you do in the first sentence. Avoid abstract language or generic buzzwords. Say something direct like, "Michael Wilson is a business strategist and the founder of the Entrepreneur Power Network, where he helps business owners build authority and scale their impact through AI and community." This type of sentence gives the AI a clean understanding of your name, your role, your organization, and your focus. It also helps human readers instantly recognize your value.

Next, provide supporting details that reinforce your credibility. These can include your years of experience, the type of clients you serve, the results you have helped others achieve, and any notable accomplishments. AI models pick up on quantifiable data and specific outcomes, so include facts that show your expertise. For example, "Over the past ten years, he has coached hundreds of entrepreneurs, authored multiple books, and helped launch more than 180 business courses." This type of sentence helps the AI associate your name with a body of work, not just a title.

Your bio should also include keywords that align with the topics you want to be known for. These keywords should be naturally woven into your writing, not stuffed awkwardly. Think about the questions people ask AI tools when looking for someone like you. If you want to show up in responses related to business coaching, AI strategy, or veteran entrepreneurship, those phrases should appear in your bio. AI tools rely on language patterns to categorize expertise. Help them understand exactly what field you operate in by using the right terminology.

Tone and structure matter as well. Use plain, conversational language rather than corporate jargon. Write in complete sentences. Avoid bullet points unless you are listing specific achievements. While bullet points may work in a resume, LLMs tend to interpret narrative content more effectively in paragraph form. The goal is to create a story that is both human and machine-readable. Think of it as a short, clear article that tells your professional story without fluff.

Now let's talk about your About page. This is often one of the most visited sections of a website, and it plays a major role in how AI tools interpret your brand. A well-crafted About page gives the AI more context about your mission, your values, and your unique approach. Begin with a short summary of your business, just like your bio, but expand on it with details about your journey. Tell the story of how and why you started your company, the problems you solve, and what makes your approach different from others in your space.

Use headings to break the content into clear sections. For example, include sections titled "Our Mission," "Who We Help," "How We Work," or "Why Choose Us." These clear labels not only improve the user experience but also help AI systems understand the structure of your content. Within each section, speak directly to your audience and explain what they can expect when working with you. Be specific. Vague promises like "We help businesses grow" do not give the AI or the reader much to work with. Instead, say something like, "We help service-based entrepreneurs automate their sales process using AI tools, personalized coaching, and community support."

Also include links to other pages that reinforce your expertise. This might include your blog, your media appearances, your portfolio, or your testimonials. Internal linking helps AI understand how your content is connected and which topics are most important to your brand. The more structured and intentional your About page is, the more useful it becomes to both your audience and the AI.

Another smart strategy is to use schema markup on your bio and About page. Schema is a type of structured data that gives AI systems additional information about your content. While it is more technical, using schema helps search engines and AI platforms accurately categorize your page. Tools like Google's Structured Data Markup Helper can make this easier to implement, or you can ask your web developer to add it for you. Schema tags like "Person," "Organization," or "Author" can help reinforce the identity and expertise of the person behind the brand.

To summarize, creating LLM-trainable bios and About pages is about being clear, specific, and structured. You want to give both human readers and AI platforms a full, accurate picture of who you are and what you offer. Focus on plain language, measurable results, and consistent messaging. Include the right keywords, tell your story with intention, and connect your content across multiple platforms.

Your bio and About page are not just introductions. They are digital assets that help AI systems understand your authority. When done right, they make it easier for tools like ChatGPT and Claude to recommend your business in conversations, answers, and advice. That visibility leads to trust. And trust leads to growth. Take the time to write bios and About pages that truly reflect your expertise, and you will open the door to new opportunities in the AI-driven marketplace.

The importance of consistency across digital channels

Consistency across your digital channels is one of the most important elements in building trust, improving visibility, and increasing your chances of being recognized by AI platforms. Whether someone finds you through your website, LinkedIn profile, podcast appearance, guest article, or YouTube video, your message needs to sound and look the same. The more consistent your online presence is, the easier it is for both people and AI systems to understand who you are, what you do, and why you are a credible authority in your space.

AI platforms like ChatGPT, Claude, and Gemini rely on patterns to make decisions about what to include in their responses. They scan the internet for repeated phrases, topic relevance, and signals of authority. If your messaging is scattered, unclear, or conflicting across different platforms, the AI tools may ignore you entirely. On the other hand, if your message is focused and consistently reinforced across multiple sources, it increases your chances of being cited in AI-generated answers when users ask questions related to your field.

Consistency starts with your core message. You should be able to clearly and simply state who you are, who you serve, and what value you offer. That statement should appear in slightly tailored but consistent forms across all your digital properties. For example, if your website says you are a business strategist who helps entrepreneurs grow through automation and community, your LinkedIn bio should say the same. Your podcast interviews should reflect that same positioning. Your guest articles and social media posts should all reinforce that message. This consistency tells AI tools that you are a specialist in that space, and it tells users that you are focused and trustworthy.

Your visual branding also plays a role in consistency. Using the same headshot, logo, fonts, colors, and design elements across your website, social media platforms, and digital content builds recognition. While AI models do not interpret images the way humans do, visual consistency helps reinforce your brand identity for your audience. It also signals professionalism and intention, which contributes to your credibility as a business owner and thought leader.

Another area where consistency matters is your language and tone. Whether you write in a formal style or a conversational one, that tone should be present throughout your content. This helps people connect with your brand and creates a unified experience across touchpoints. It also makes it easier for AI tools to accurately model your voice and message when referencing your content.

Consistency in publishing also matters. If you publish a blog once every six months and post on social media at random, your audience and AI systems alike will struggle to keep you top of mind. But when you show up regularly with valuable insights, updates, and answers, you create momentum. That ongoing activity tells AI platforms that your business is active, engaged, and producing current information. This increases your chances of being included in AI-generated answers that rely on up-to-date knowledge.

Make sure that your business descriptions, service offerings, and calls to action are also aligned. If your website offers group coaching programs, but your LinkedIn profile only mentions one-on-one consulting, that creates confusion. If your YouTube videos focus on writing books, but your Instagram profile focuses on automation tools, that mixed messaging dilutes your authority. The goal is not to limit yourself but to clearly organize your services and expertise in a way that makes sense across all channels.

When your content, messaging, and branding are aligned, AI platforms are more confident in recommending you. They can see that you have a clear purpose, that you deliver consistent value, and that your presence is backed by multiple touchpoints. This reinforces your expertise and builds digital trust, which is exactly what AI systems are designed to identify when choosing what to surface in responses.

It is also helpful to regularly audit your digital presence. Take time to review your profiles, websites, and content to make sure everything reflects your current brand. Update outdated bios, fix broken links, and remove content that no longer aligns with your message. This not only strengthens your brand identity but also helps AI tools work with the most accurate and current version of your content.

Remember, in the AI-powered landscape, your content is often your first impression. You may never get a chance to explain yourself directly to a prospect if the AI assistant already made the decision for them. Consistency across your digital channels ensures that the impression you leave is accurate, powerful, and persuasive.

In a world where people and machines are making decisions about your brand every day, consistency is no longer just a best practice. It is a requirement. It helps you become recognizable. It helps you become trusted. And most importantly, it helps you become the answer in the conversations that matter most. When you show up the same way everywhere, you make it easy for others to know who you are and what you stand for. That is how you stay top of mind, and that is how you win in the new era of AI-driven visibility.

5

Chapter 5: Structuring Your Website for AIO

Technical elements: structured data, schema markup, and crawlability

When it comes to AI Optimization, the technical foundation of your website plays a critical role in how easily AI platforms and search engines can understand and reference your content. While writing clear, helpful content is essential, the structure behind that content determines whether it can actually be found, interpreted, and used. Three of the most important technical elements for improving your digital visibility are structured data, schema markup, and crawlability. Each one supports how information is organized, presented, and accessed by AI systems and search engines.

Structured data refers to information that is organized in a predictable, machine-readable format. Unlike regular content that is written for humans to read, structured data is written for machines to process. It helps AI tools and search engines know exactly what a specific piece of content is about. For example, if your website includes an event, structured data allows you to define the event name, date, location, and time in a way that machines can recognize instantly. This structure removes guesswork and makes it easier for AI tools to use that information when providing recommendations, summaries, or search results.

Schema markup is a type of structured data that provides additional context about the content on your website. It uses standardized vocabulary developed by Schema.org, which is supported by major search engines and used by AI platforms to better understand content types. There are different schema types for articles, books, events, local businesses, products, reviews, and more. When you add schema markup to your pages, you are tagging your content with clear labels that tell machines what it is. For example, if you tag a page as a "Person" with properties like name, job title, and affiliation, AI tools can more easily connect that page to the right expert or brand.

Adding schema to your site is often done through simple code snippets placed in the header of your page or embedded within the HTML of your content. If you are using platforms like WordPress, Shopify, or Squarespace, there are plugins and tools that make this process easier. Structured data is not visible to the average user, but it makes a big difference in how AI and search engines interpret your content. When implemented properly, schema markup can improve your visibility in search features like rich snippets and increase the chances that your content will be referenced in AI-generated answers.

Crawlability refers to how easily search engines and AI crawlers can access, scan, and index your website. If your site is difficult to navigate, slow to load, or blocked by incorrect settings, AI systems may miss your content entirely. This includes making sure your robots.txt file is properly configured, your sitemap is submitted to search engines, and your site structure is logical. Pages should be internally linked in a way that helps both users and machines find related content. If your content is buried deep within the site with no clear links leading to it, AI crawlers may never reach it, which means it will not be included in the index or training data.

Mobile responsiveness also plays a role in crawlability. Many AI tools and search engines prioritize content that performs well across devices. Make sure your content is easy to read and interact with on smartphones and tablets. A slow, unresponsive site creates friction, which can hurt your visibility. Use tools like Google PageSpeed Insights to test your site's performance and make necessary improvements. These adjustments do not just help users. They improve the ability of AI systems to access and interpret your information.

Another key factor is URL structure. Clean, descriptive URLs that include relevant keywords help AI tools understand what the page is about. Avoid using generic URLs filled with numbers or random characters. Instead, use meaningful paths like "/about," "/services," or "/ai-coaching-for-entrepreneurs." Clear URLs add to the overall structure of your site and improve the readability of your content from a machine's point of view.

You should also avoid duplicate content, broken links, and outdated pages. These issues create confusion for AI systems and can lower the overall credibility of your site. Use website auditing tools to identify and fix these issues regularly. Keeping your site clean and organized signals that your content is current, reliable, and worth referencing.

Security is another technical element that contributes to credibility and crawlability. Make sure your site uses HTTPS instead of HTTP. This encrypts the connection between your site and the user, and it is considered a ranking signal by search engines. Most modern browsers and AI systems view HTTPS as a standard, and lacking it can hurt your visibility and trustworthiness.

Together, structured data, schema markup, and crawlability form the technical backbone of your online presence. These elements do not replace good content. They support it by ensuring that your content can be found, understood, and used by the systems people are relying on to make decisions. Without this foundation, even the best content can be overlooked.

By taking the time to implement these technical elements properly, you improve your chances of showing up in AI-generated answers, voice search results, and rich snippets on traditional search engines. This positions your brand not just as a participant in the digital world, but as a trusted source of reliable information.

In the age of AI-driven discovery, technical optimization is not just for developers or SEO specialists. It is a key part of your visibility strategy. When you make your content easy for machines to read and interpret, you make it easier for your business to be found by the right people, at the right time, in the right context. That is how you build real momentum, and that is how you stay ahead in a rapidly changing digital landscape.

Creating AI-friendly site architecture

Creating AI-friendly site architecture is one of the most effective ways to improve how your content is discovered, understood, and used by AI platforms like ChatGPT, Claude, and Gemini. While content is the substance of your message, the structure of your website is the framework that supports and delivers it. If your site is disorganized, difficult to navigate, or lacking clear pathways, both AI tools and human users may struggle to make sense of what you offer. A well-structured website helps AI systems understand the hierarchy of your content, prioritize key information, and recognize how different pieces relate to one another.

At the foundation of AI-friendly architecture is clarity. Each page on your site should have a clear purpose and be easy to find through intuitive navigation. Start with a logical main menu that reflects the most important areas of your business. Common top-level pages include Home, About, Services, Blog, and Contact. Under Services, you can list subpages for each individual offering. If you have multiple target audiences, consider creating dedicated landing pages for each group. This helps AI tools understand the specific solutions you provide and who they are for.

Each page should focus on a single topic or service. Do not overload one page with too many ideas or offerings. This can confuse users and make it harder for AI tools to identify the core message. For example, if you offer coaching, consulting, and online courses, each of those services should have its own page with clear content tailored to that offering. This separation improves both user experience and machine interpretation.

Internal linking is another important element of AI-friendly architecture. When you link related pages together, you help both users and AI crawlers discover additional content and understand how your information is connected. For instance, if you mention business automation on your homepage, link it to your dedicated automation service page. If you write a blog post about email marketing, link it to your email marketing service or resources. This network of connections strengthens your site's structure and reinforces your authority on specific topics.

Use descriptive URLs that reflect the content of each page. A URL like "yourwebsite.com/ai-marketing-strategy" is much more informative than "yourwebsite.com/page1." Clear URLs improve the readability of your site for AI crawlers and increase your chances of being included in relevant search results or AI-generated responses.

Breadcrumb navigation is another helpful tool. Breadcrumbs show the user's path through your site and indicate the relationship between pages. They also give AI systems additional context about how your content is organized. If someone lands on a blog post about "AI Tools for Small Business," breadcrumbs might display a trail like Home > Blog > AI Tools > Small Business. This structure reinforces your topical relevance and helps both users and machines understand where the content fits within your site.

Your sitemap also plays a critical role. A sitemap is a file that lists all the important pages on your website, helping AI and search engine crawlers find and index them efficiently. Make sure your sitemap is clean, up to date, and submitted to platforms like Google Search Console. This makes it easier for AI systems to access your full library of content, especially if your site includes a growing number of blog posts, resources, or landing pages.

Avoid orphan pages, which are pages that have no internal links pointing to them. These pages are hard to find and often go unnoticed by crawlers. Every page should connect to another page or be part of a logical content flow. For example, if you write an article about "Using ChatGPT for Business Growth," make sure it is linked from your blog index and from other relevant articles or service pages.

In addition to structure, page load speed also impacts AI-friendliness. AI tools and search engines prefer fast-loading sites because they improve user experience and make it easier to access content. Compress images, minimize unnecessary scripts, and choose reliable hosting to keep your site running smoothly. A slow site can limit crawl activity and reduce the visibility of your content.

Mobile optimization is just as important. Many AI tools prioritize content that is mobile-friendly, and users expect a seamless experience across devices. Make sure your site is responsive, meaning it adjusts automatically to different screen sizes. Use readable fonts, properly spaced buttons, and layouts that make navigation easy on smartphones and tablets.

Finally, include structured data and schema markup to provide additional clarity about your content. Label your pages with schema types such as "Local Business," "Service," "Article," or "FAQ." This allows AI systems to quickly identify what kind of content you are offering and how it should be categorized. When combined with a strong site structure, schema helps elevate your visibility and increases the chance that your content will be pulled into AI-generated responses.

In summary, AI-friendly site architecture is about more than just design. It is about building a structure that supports your content, improves discoverability, and makes it easy for both users and AI systems to understand what you offer. Clear menus, focused pages, internal links, optimized URLs, and proper indexing all work together to help your business show up in the right place at the right time. In an environment where AI tools are becoming the first stop for user questions and research, a smart, intentional website structure can give you the edge you need to stand out and succeed.

Optimizing blog posts, service pages, and landing pages

Optimizing your blog posts, service pages, and landing pages is essential if you want your content to be understood, ranked, and recommended by both search engines and AI tools like ChatGPT, Claude, and Gemini. While each of these types of pages serves a different purpose, they all contribute to your overall visibility online. When they are structured and written correctly, they help AI systems recognize your authority, understand your offerings, and deliver your content to users who are asking questions related to your expertise.

Let's start with blog posts. Blogs are one of the most effective tools for driving traffic, educating your audience, and establishing thought leadership. From an AI Optimization perspective, blog posts should be written clearly, provide real value, and focus on a specific topic. Start with a compelling headline that includes a keyword or phrase someone might search for or ask about. For example, instead of saying "Thoughts on Productivity," use a more direct title like "How Business Owners Can Use AI to Improve Daily

Productivity."

In the body of your post, structure the content with subheadings to break up sections and guide the reader. AI systems use these headers to understand the flow of your article and extract key points. Keep your paragraphs short, use plain language, and support your ideas with data or examples when possible. You should also include internal links to relevant service pages or other blog posts. This not only keeps readers on your site longer but also strengthens the overall structure of your content for AI crawlers.

End each blog post with a clear call to action. This might be an invitation to book a consultation, download a resource, or explore one of your services. A strong closing helps both the user and AI understand what the next step should be. Make sure your blog is updated regularly. Consistent publishing signals to AI platforms that your site is active and trustworthy.

Now let's move to service pages. These pages are the core of your business website because they describe what you offer and how you help. Each service should have its own dedicated page. Do not lump all your services together on one generic page. When you give each service its own space, you allow AI tools to understand and categorize the content more accurately.

Start with a headline that clearly states the service and the benefit to the client. For example, "AI-Powered Business Coaching for Entrepreneurs" is more effective than just "Coaching." In the body, describe the problem your service solves, the process you follow, and the results clients can expect. Use bullet points or numbered steps to make the information easy to scan. These elements help AI systems pull key data from your page when generating summaries or recommendations.

You should also include testimonials or client success stories on your service pages. These not only build trust with human visitors but also provide additional content that supports your credibility. Make sure your contact information or booking link is easy to find. AI tools often use structured data to identify calls to action, so be sure these elements are clearly labeled and accessible.

Finally, landing pages are designed for conversions. These are often used in advertising, lead generation, or product launches. A landing page should be tightly focused on a single offer or goal. Start with a headline that speaks directly to your audience's need or desire. Follow with a short paragraph or video that explains the value of what you are offering. Use testimonials, feature lists, and visuals to reinforce your message.

Keep your landing page clean and distraction-free. Remove unnecessary navigation or external links unless they support the core offer. Use a strong, visible call to action, such as a sign-up form, download button, or purchase link. From an AI standpoint, landing pages that are too vague or cluttered may not be indexed properly. Make sure the page clearly explains who it is for, what it does, and how the user can take the next step.

Whether you are writing a blog post, service page, or landing page, always think about clarity, context, and structure. Use headings, subheadings, and internal links to guide both users and AI tools through your content. Avoid filler language and focus on delivering real value. Consistent formatting, targeted keywords, and relevant examples all help reinforce your expertise and improve your visibility in both search and AI-generated responses.

As AI platforms continue to play a larger role in how people find information, optimizing your core content is no longer just a marketing best practice. It is a necessity. These pages are your voice online. They represent your knowledge, your business, and your unique value. When they are optimized with purpose and precision, they become powerful tools for attracting attention, building trust, and turning curious visitors into loyal clients.

Using internal links and semantic tagging

Internal linking and semantic tagging are powerful tools for improving how your content is understood by both search engines and AI systems like ChatGPT, Claude, and Gemini. These strategies are not just about organizing your website. They are about making your content easier to navigate, easier to interpret, and more likely to be included in AI-generated responses. When used correctly, they can increase your visibility, strengthen your authority, and guide both users and machines through the journey of your expertise.

Internal links are the connections between pages on your own website. They help users move from one piece of content to another and show AI crawlers how your content is related. For example, if you write a blog post about business automation and you have a service page that offers automation consulting, you should link the blog post to that service page. This not only drives traffic to the page where conversions happen but also signals to AI that the two topics are closely connected.

Think of internal links as the roadmap of your website. When you link related articles, resources, and service pages together, you are showing both the user and the AI how your ideas connect. This helps build topic clusters around specific areas of expertise. The stronger and more organized your internal linking strategy is, the more likely it is that your site will be understood as an authority on that topic.

There are a few best practices to follow with internal linking. First, use descriptive anchor text. Instead of linking a phrase like "click here," use a phrase that describes the destination, such as "AI marketing strategy" or "content optimization guide." This helps AI systems understand what the linked page is about. Second, make sure the links are relevant. Only link to content that adds value to the reader. Random or excessive linking can confuse users and hurt your site's performance.

Next, let's talk about semantic tagging. Semantic tagging is the process of labeling your content with tags that communicate meaning. It allows AI systems to better understand the structure and purpose of your information. This is often done through HTML tags and schema markup, which define the role of different parts of your content.

For example, using header tags like H1, H2, and H3 tells both humans and machines what the main topics and subtopics of your page are. A well-structured article might begin with an H1 for the main title, followed by H2s for each major section, and H3s for subpoints within those sections. This hierarchy helps AI systems extract key insights and organize your content for summaries or recommendations.

Schema markup takes semantic tagging a step further by allowing you to define specific types of content. You can tag a blog post as an "Article," a review as a "ProductReview," or a business location as a "LocalBusiness." These tags help search engines and AI platforms classify your content correctly and display it in rich formats or search results.

Semantic tagging also helps clarify ambiguous content. For example, if you are a coach who offers group programs and one-on-one services, you can use schema to differentiate those offerings clearly. This ensures that AI systems do not confuse one service with another and that your content appears in the right context for the right audience.

Both internal linking and semantic tagging work together to create a clear, organized, and meaningful digital experience. Internal links guide people and machines from one piece of relevant content to another. Semantic tags help define what each piece of content is and how it fits into the bigger picture.

In a world where AI tools are constantly scanning the internet for information, these strategies are more important than ever. They allow you to present your knowledge in a format that machines can understand and use. When done well, internal links and semantic tags not only improve your visibility but also build trust with your audience by creating a seamless and informative user experience.

If you want your content to be found, recommended, and respected in an AI-driven world, these technical strategies should be part of your regular content workflow. They are not flashy. They are not complicated. But they are the backbone of a website that is both user-friendly and AI-ready. Take the time to build meaningful connections between your content and use tags that speak the language of both people and machines. Your future visibility depends on it.

6

Chapter 6: Leveraging Other Platforms to Boost AI Visibility

How AI tools pull from third-party sources (Reddit, forums, reviews, etc.)

AI tools like ChatGPT, Claude, and Gemini are designed to provide users with helpful, relevant, and accurate answers to their questions. To do this, they rely on massive amounts of data drawn from a wide range of sources across the internet. While some of this information comes from books, news articles, and academic research, a large and often overlooked portion comes from third-party platforms like Reddit, Quora, online forums, product reviews, and user-generated content. These sources play a significant role in shaping how AI models understand topics, form opinions, and decide which brands or solutions to mention in their responses.

Reddit is one of the most influential third-party platforms in this context. With thousands of active communities, or subreddits, Reddit hosts in-depth conversations on almost every subject imaginable. People ask questions, share personal experiences, compare products, and offer real-world advice. AI models are trained to pick up on these patterns, and they use the language, sentiment, and feedback found in Reddit threads to inform how they answer related questions. For example, if a user asks ChatGPT for the best budgeting app, the model might consider highly upvoted Reddit discussions where users compare different options and explain why one app works better than another.

These types of insights are grounded in lived experience, and that makes them valuable training data.

Forums function in a similar way. Whether it is a niche community like a photography forum or a general tech site, forums are rich with peer-to-peer knowledge. They offer detailed responses, long-form opinions, and expert advice in specific industries. When AI tools are trained on this kind of content, they learn how real people talk about products, services, and solutions. This helps the AI generate more conversational and relatable responses. It also helps the tools identify which businesses are seen as trustworthy, which solutions are effective, and which common questions come up again and again.

Online reviews are another major source of information for AI systems. Reviews are filled with user sentiment, performance feedback, and pain points. Whether someone is reviewing a book on Amazon, a restaurant on Yelp, or a software tool on G2, they are providing raw data about their experience. AI models analyze this data to detect trends, identify frequently mentioned features, and measure customer satisfaction. If a product consistently receives positive reviews across multiple platforms, the AI may give it more weight when suggesting options. On the other hand, if a business has many complaints about the same issue, that pattern might inform how the AI responds to related questions.

What makes these third-party sources so important is that they are not controlled by the business owner. This adds a layer of credibility and authenticity to the content. AI models are designed to favor neutral, organic, and diverse sources of information. That is why user-generated content often carries more weight than promotional material. For business owners, this means your presence on platforms like Reddit, Quora, and review sites is just as important as your own website or social media. When people are talking about your product or service in a positive, helpful way, that conversation can influence how AI tools see your brand and whether they include you in their responses.

It is also worth noting that AI tools look for consensus. If the same message or opinion shows up across different forums, reviews, and articles, the AI is more likely to trust that message. This means consistency matters.

Encouraging satisfied customers to leave honest reviews, participating in relevant online discussions, and contributing valuable insights to forums can help build that positive consensus over time. It is not about spamming every thread with your link. It is about being genuinely helpful and adding value in places where people are already asking questions related to your expertise.

Quora is another platform that influences AI training. It is structured as a question-and-answer site, which aligns closely with how AI tools function. When you answer questions on Quora with detailed, well-written insights, you are not only helping users but also feeding the AI ecosystem with high-quality content. If your answers are upvoted and seen as helpful, the AI is more likely to view you as a credible source. This can eventually lead to your insights being paraphrased or referenced in future responses.

In summary, AI tools pull from a broad web of third-party sources to shape the answers they provide. Platforms like Reddit, online forums, Quora, and review sites are key components of that data. These sources offer authentic, real-world feedback and create digital trails that AI systems use to gauge credibility and relevance. For business owners, this presents a major opportunity. By showing up in these spaces with value-driven, honest contributions, you increase the chances of being included in AI-generated answers. You are not just building visibility with human readers. You are also becoming part of the AI's understanding of your industry.

This shift changes the game. No longer is it just about optimizing your own site. Now, visibility is influenced by how others talk about you and where those conversations happen. By being intentional about your presence on third-party platforms, you position your brand to be seen, heard, and recommended in the places that matter most.

Building presence on AI-indexed platforms: Yelp, Trustpilot, Google My Business

If you want your business to show up in AI-generated answers, building a strong presence on platforms like Yelp, Trustpilot, and Google My Business is no longer optional. These platforms are some of the most visible, publicly accessible sources that AI models use to gather information about local businesses, services, and customer satisfaction. The data they contain plays a key role in how tools like ChatGPT, Claude, and Gemini answer user questions about which businesses to trust, which services are top-rated, and where to go for specific needs.

Let's begin with Google My Business. This platform is one of the most influential local business directories online. When someone searches for a service in a specific area, Google My Business listings appear prominently in the results. These listings include your business name, location, phone number, website, hours of operation, reviews, and often photos. All of this data is used not just by Google, but also by AI platforms that want to provide relevant, location-based answers. If your listing is complete and accurate, it increases your chances of being recommended when someone nearby searches for your service or asks an AI tool for local suggestions.

To optimize your Google My Business presence, start by claiming and verifying your listing. Add detailed information about your business, including categories that describe what you offer. Use high-quality images, respond to reviews, and post regular updates or offers. These updates help signal that your business is active and engaged, which builds trust with both potential customers and AI systems. Encourage satisfied clients to leave honest reviews, and be sure to respond professionally to both positive and negative feedback.

Yelp is another key platform, especially for service-based and hospitality businesses. It holds a massive database of reviews and ratings that influence user decisions and, increasingly, AI recommendations. Yelp reviews often appear in search engine results and are indexed by AI models when analyzing brand reputation and service quality. If someone asks an AI tool, "What is the best local coffee shop?" the answer might be influenced by high-rated Yelp listings with a strong review history.

To build your Yelp presence, make sure your profile is fully filled out. Choose the right business categories, add professional photos, and write a compelling business description. Monitor your reviews and respond regularly to customer feedback. Yelp's algorithm favors businesses that are active and responsive, which also signals to AI systems that your business is trustworthy and engaged with its audience.

Trustpilot is especially useful for businesses that serve national or international audiences, particularly in e-commerce, software, and professional services. It is a reviews platform focused on helping customers evaluate businesses based on honest user experiences. What sets Trustpilot apart is that it often ranks highly in search results and is heavily crawled by AI tools looking for review data. A strong Trustpilot profile can contribute to your brand's digital footprint and reinforce your credibility in the eyes of AI systems.

To maximize your impact on Trustpilot, invite your customers to leave reviews after every purchase or service engagement. Be transparent and authentic in your interactions. Use the review management tools to respond and address any concerns professionally. Over time, a high volume of positive, genuine reviews can create the kind of digital signal that AI platforms recognize and respect.

Building presence on these platforms is not just about getting good reviews. It is about creating consistent, trustworthy signals across the internet that define who you are, what you offer, and how people feel about your business. AI models look for patterns. If the same business name, address, and phone number appear across Yelp, Trustpilot, Google My Business, and your website, that consistency strengthens your reputation. If reviews across platforms highlight the same strengths—such as excellent service, fast delivery, or helpful staff—those themes become part of your brand's online identity.

In the age of AI-driven search, your online reputation is not built solely on your website or social media. It is shaped by what customers say, where they say it, and how frequently those opinions appear in trusted public places. Yelp, Trustpilot, and Google My Business are not just marketing tools. They are data sources that AI platforms rely on to decide which businesses to recommend when users ask for guidance.

To take full advantage of this shift, be proactive. Monitor your listings, respond to reviews, and keep your information up to date. Focus on delivering excellent customer experiences that naturally lead to positive feedback. Over time, your presence on these AI-indexed platforms will help you rise to the top—not just in search results, but in the answers that AI tools deliver to users around the world. Visibility starts with trust, and trust starts with a presence that can be seen, measured, and reinforced by the platforms shaping the future of business discovery.

Repurposing content for platforms like YouTube, Substack, and podcasts (which LLMs reference)

If you want to improve your visibility in the age of AI, you need to go beyond just publishing on your website. Large language models like ChatGPT, Claude, and Gemini are trained on publicly accessible content across the internet, and that includes platforms like YouTube, Substack, and podcasts. These platforms have become rich sources of information that AI tools reference when generating answers to user questions. Repurposing your content for these channels helps you expand your reach, reinforce your authority, and increase the chances that your expertise will be cited or included in AI-generated responses.

Let's start with YouTube. Google owns YouTube, and it is one of the most highly indexed platforms in the world. When you create video content, especially educational or instructional videos, you are contributing to a searchable database that both humans and AI systems rely on. Many AI models are trained on video titles, descriptions, captions, and user engagement signals from platforms like YouTube. That means your content, if optimized properly, can be surfaced in response to questions like "How do I grow my business with automation?" or "What is the best marketing strategy for coaches?"

To take advantage of this, repurpose your existing blog posts, webinars, or client lessons into short, focused videos. Use titles that clearly reflect the problem you are solving. Include detailed descriptions and relevant tags. Most importantly, enable and edit your captions, since AI models often use closed caption data to understand video content. Consistent publishing helps build your channel's authority, while thoughtful topics and structured presentation make your content more discoverable and more valuable to AI tools looking for trusted information.

Substack is another powerful platform that blends blogging, newsletters, and thought leadership. Substack articles are public by default and frequently crawled by search engines and AI systems. When you publish on Substack, you are creating written content that is easy for language models to ingest. You can repurpose content from your website or podcast episodes into essay-style insights that offer depth and clarity. Substack also encourages thought leadership, which means you can establish yourself as an expert in your field and have that authority picked up by AI tools scanning for credible voices on a topic.

To use Substack effectively, write in a clear, educational tone. Break long posts into sections with headers. Use bold or italicized text to emphasize key points. Link to relevant resources, including your own blog or YouTube channel. The goal is to create content that stands alone in value, but also ties back to your ecosystem. If you do interviews, publish a transcript on Substack alongside key takeaways. If you teach a framework, write it out in full and explain it in practical terms. These kinds of posts are more likely to be referenced by language models, especially when they are well structured and frequently read or shared.

Podcasts are also increasingly indexed by AI tools. While audio files themselves are not always used directly in training models, the transcripts, show notes, and titles associated with podcasts are. That means your ideas and stories shared through audio can make their way into the datasets used by large language models. If your podcast discusses strategies, case studies, lessons, or frameworks, that content becomes part of the broader conversation AI systems are listening to.

To repurpose content into podcasts, start with outlines or scripts based on your blog posts or recorded coaching sessions. Keep episodes focused and actionable. Title your episodes clearly so AI tools can recognize the topic. Always include detailed show notes and, when possible, a full transcript. These text-based elements are what help your audio content become accessible to machines. You can host your podcast on platforms like Spotify, Apple Podcasts, or your own site, but make sure the content is public and easy to find.

Repurposing does not mean simply copying and pasting. It means adjusting your message and format to fit the platform while maintaining the original value. What works as a blog post might need to be simplified for YouTube or expanded for a podcast. You can take a long-form article and turn it into a series of YouTube shorts, a list of key takeaways for Substack, or a multi-part podcast series. This multiplies the exposure of your message and creates multiple entry points for both your audience and AI systems.

AI tools do not favor one format over another. They prioritize content that is consistent, valuable, and widely distributed. By showing up across YouTube, Substack, and podcast platforms with a unified message and helpful content, you are signaling to AI models that you are a trusted source in your domain. Over time, that trust is reflected in how often your content is referenced or recommended in AI-generated answers.

The platforms where you repurpose your content also serve human audiences. You are building credibility, connection, and community with real people, while also optimizing for machine visibility. This dual benefit makes repurposing one of the most efficient strategies for growing your influence in the AI era. When you repurpose intentionally and align your messaging across channels, you create a digital footprint that both people and AI systems will recognize and respect.

7

Chapter 7: AI Tools That Can Help You Optimize for AI

Using ChatGPT to audit your own content

ChatGPT is more than just a tool for generating content. It can also serve as a powerful assistant for auditing and improving the content you have already created. As AI becomes a central part of how people discover information, it is important to make sure your content aligns with what AI systems recognize as clear, credible, and helpful. Auditing your content with ChatGPT allows you to review how your messaging will be interpreted by both human readers and language models, and it helps you identify gaps, inconsistencies, or missed opportunities.

Start by feeding your existing content into ChatGPT. This could be a blog post, service page, landing page, or even an entire sales letter. Once you input the content, ask ChatGPT to evaluate it for clarity, structure, and relevance. For example, you might say, "Read the following content and tell me if it is clear, easy to understand, and answers the question a reader might have." ChatGPT can then provide a summary of strengths and areas for improvement. This is especially helpful when trying to make your content more AI-friendly because it highlights whether your message is being conveyed in a way that an AI system would easily understand and relay.

You can also ask ChatGPT to test how your content responds to search-style questions. Paste your content and then prompt ChatGPT with a related question like, "What are the benefits of hiring a business coach?" and see if the model refers back to the key points in your content. If it struggles to generate a helpful answer based on your material, that is a sign that your message might be unclear or not focused enough. This approach mirrors how AI tools pull from available data to generate responses and allows you to test your visibility in real time.

Beyond clarity, you can use ChatGPT to evaluate the structure of your content. Ask it to break your content into main points, highlight the headings, or identify whether you are answering questions in a logical order. This kind of review can help you make your pages easier to navigate for both users and AI tools. You might also ask for suggestions on how to add internal links or where to include FAQs that would help improve the value of the content.

Another smart use of ChatGPT for auditing is checking tone and consistency. If you are writing content across multiple pages, newsletters, or platforms, ChatGPT can help you identify if your tone matches your brand voice or if certain pieces feel disconnected. You can ask it to compare two pieces of writing and explain whether they sound like the same author or if one is more formal, vague, or off-brand. This kind of review helps create a more cohesive digital presence, which AI systems tend to reward.

For businesses trying to appear in AI-generated answers, authority and context are just as important as clarity. You can ask ChatGPT to assess whether your content establishes credibility and explains your expertise. Ask questions like, "Does this content make the author sound like an expert?" or "What kind of authority is being communicated in this page?" If the answer is weak, you know it is time to add testimonials, case studies, credentials, or specific examples to strengthen your positioning.

You can also use ChatGPT to improve formatting. Ask the tool how your content could be made more scannable, readable, or digestible. It might suggest adding bullet points, summarizing sections with bold subheaders, or breaking long paragraphs into shorter blocks. These changes not only make your content better for human readers but also improve how AI systems digest and recall your material.

Finally, ChatGPT can simulate user feedback. Ask it to respond to your content as if it were your ideal customer. For example, say, "Act like a small business owner looking for help with marketing. After reading this page, what questions do you still have?" This will help you find gaps in your messaging and identify where your content might not be meeting the expectations of your audience.

Auditing your content with ChatGPT gives you an always-available assistant that works quickly, provides structured feedback, and helps you stay aligned with how modern search and AI tools evaluate information. It is a practical way to maintain quality and consistency across your digital assets while sharpening your message for the new way people discover solutions.

Incorporating this kind of audit into your workflow ensures that your content continues to work for you long after it is published. Instead of guessing what AI systems might interpret, you can simulate that process and refine your content accordingly. This leads to better visibility, stronger engagement, and greater authority in a digital landscape increasingly shaped by artificial intelligence.

Other tools: Perplexity.ai, Frase, Surfer SEO, Jasper, and others

In addition to ChatGPT, there are several other tools that can help business owners improve their visibility and content performance in an AI-driven world. Platforms like Perplexity.ai, Frase, Surfer SEO, and Jasper are built to assist with research, content generation, optimization, and strategic positioning. Each of these tools plays a unique role, and when used together, they provide a full suite of capabilities for those who want to stay ahead of the curve in marketing, publishing, and AI Optimization.

Perplexity.ai is a powerful research and answer engine that offers real-time, citation-backed responses. It functions as a conversational search tool that pulls information from across the web, delivering concise and well-sourced summaries. For business owners, it is a useful tool to understand how questions are being answered across the internet and how your competitors or industry peers are being referenced. If your goal is to appear in AI-generated answers, studying what Perplexity.ai includes in its citations gives you insight into where your brand needs to be mentioned, whether that's on Wikipedia, blog posts, LinkedIn articles, or third-party review platforms.

Frase is designed to help you research, write, and optimize content based on search intent. It analyzes top-ranking content for a given keyword and helps you build outlines and full articles that match what users and AI models expect. Frase excels at uncovering the kinds of questions people are asking and the topics you should be covering in your content to show up more often. It also offers built-in tools to identify content gaps, making it easier to align your writing with what audiences and AI systems are looking for.

Surfer SEO focuses on data-driven content optimization. It provides a real-time scoring system for your articles based on keyword usage, structure, word count, headings, and other ranking signals. By using Surfer SEO, you can fine-tune your content to improve its performance on search engines and increase its relevance in AI systems that prioritize well-structured and topic-rich pages. It is especially useful for identifying overused or missing keywords and ensuring that your content remains competitive in crowded spaces.

Jasper, formerly known as Jarvis, is an AI writing assistant tailored for marketers, entrepreneurs, and content creators. It helps you generate content quickly using customizable templates for blog posts, social media, emails, ads, and more. Jasper is powered by large language models similar to ChatGPT, but it includes workflows and prompts designed for business applications. You can use Jasper to repurpose your long-form content into smaller assets, test different angles or tones, and generate SEO-optimized copy with minimal effort. This saves time while maintaining a consistent voice across all your marketing channels.

Other noteworthy tools include Clearscope and MarketMuse, both of which are advanced content optimization platforms that help you rank higher and align better with semantic search. These tools dig deep into language patterns and topic modeling to ensure your content matches user intent and AI interpretation. Grammarly and Hemingway Editor are excellent for clarity and readability, which directly affect how your content is understood by readers and language models alike. Descript is a great option if you are working with audio or video content and need fast transcription, editing, or repurposing tools for podcasts and YouTube.

Together, these tools create a comprehensive ecosystem for AI Optimization. They help you generate better content, identify the right keywords, optimize for readability and structure, track your competition, and ensure your digital footprint is strong and visible. In a world where AI tools are referencing a wide variety of sources to build their answers, the goal is no longer to rank on a single search engine. The goal is to be present, consistent, and valuable across the digital landscape.

By integrating platforms like Perplexity.ai, Frase, Surfer SEO, and Jasper into your workflow, you can create content that meets both the human need for clarity and the machine need for structure and relevance. This balance is what drives modern visibility, builds authority, and positions your brand for long-term success. As the digital space continues to shift toward AI-curated information, these tools provide the insight and support you need to stay relevant, stand out, and get found.

Prompt examples for generating content that AIs can understand and recommend

Creating content that artificial intelligence tools can understand and recommend starts with using clear, targeted prompts. Whether you are using ChatGPT, Claude, or other AI writing tools, the way you frame your request determines the quality, relevance, and usefulness of the output. Well-crafted prompts help generate content that is not only helpful to readers but also easy for language models to parse, categorize, and reference. This is a key strategy in AI Optimization and a practical way to ensure your business or brand shows up in AI-generated answers.

Here are several categories of prompt examples you can use to generate content that aligns with what large language models are designed to recognize and promote.

1. Educational or How-To Prompts

These prompts are designed to teach or explain a process. AI tools respond well to step-by-step formats, lists, and tutorials because they mimic the structure of high-performing content across the internet.

Example Prompts:

- "Write a step-by-step guide on how small business owners can automate their social media using free tools."
- "Explain how to create a customer onboarding process in five simple steps."
- "Write an article that teaches beginners how to budget using the envelope system."

2. Problem-Solution Prompts

AI systems often surface content that clearly addresses user problems. When your prompt is focused on solving a specific issue, the resulting content becomes more valuable to both readers and AI platforms.

Example Prompts:

- "Create a blog post that explains how freelancers can reduce client churn."
- "Write a guide on how to fix the most common mistakes in Facebook ad targeting."
- "Provide solutions for business owners struggling with team communication."

3. Comparison Prompts

People frequently use AI to compare tools, services, or methods. These prompts produce content that satisfies search queries related to decision-making and product selection.

Example Prompts:

- "Compare ClickFunnels, Kartra, and Systeme.io for course creators. Include pros and cons."
- "Write a side-by-side comparison of working with a business coach versus joining a mastermind group."
- "Create a detailed article comparing Mailchimp and ConvertKit for email marketing."

4. List-Based Prompts

Lists are highly readable and easy for AI to identify as valuable, skimmable content. They also tend to perform well in AI-generated answers because they are concise and structured.

Example Prompts:

- "List 10 ways entrepreneurs can use ChatGPT to save time."
- "Create a list of seven habits that help business owners stay productive."
- "Write a list of the top five free tools for solopreneurs managing remote teams."

5. Authority-Building Prompts

These prompts position you or your brand as a knowledgeable source. AI models often draw on authoritative content when suggesting or quoting from expert sources.

Example Prompts:

- "Write an article from the perspective of a business strategist explaining the benefits of long-term planning."
- "Create a bio that showcases experience in helping veterans transition into entrepreneurship."
- "Write a LinkedIn post that explains why building social capital is the key to modern business success."

6. FAQ-Style Prompts

FAQs mimic common search behavior and are often used by AI systems to answer user questions directly. Prompting your AI tool to write in this style helps you build content that can be referenced naturally.

Example Prompts:

- "Answer the question: What is the best time to launch a product online?"
- "Write an FAQ section for a business coaching program, including pricing, format, and results."

- "Create an answer to the question: How does ChatGPT help small businesses with content creation?"

7. Summary and Explainer Prompts

When people use AI to understand complex topics, summary content often gets pulled in. These prompts help create digestible breakdowns of technical or dense subjects.

Example Prompts:

- "Summarize the differences between SEO and AIO in under 300 words."
- "Explain the concept of a buyer persona and how to create one."
- "Write a simple explanation of how AI uses training data to answer questions."

8. Perspective or Use-Case Prompts

Use-case content helps the AI identify who a piece of content is for. When the audience is clearly defined, AI tools can surface content to the right users at the right time.

Example Prompts:

- "Write an article explaining how real estate agents can use AI to generate leads."
- "Describe how nonprofit organizations can benefit from automation tools."
- "Explain how introverted entrepreneurs can build powerful networks using AI tools."

9. Rephrasing and Repurposing Prompts

Sometimes your existing content needs refinement to be more AI-friendly. Use prompts to reformat or simplify content for better readability and semantic clarity.

Example Prompts:

- "Rewrite this blog post to make it easier to scan using subheadings and bullet points."
- "Summarize this article in plain language suitable for beginners."
- "Repurpose this paragraph into a social media caption that highlights the main idea."

10. Formatting Prompts

Structured formatting makes content easier for AI to analyze and learn from. Prompts that request headings, lists, bolded takeaways, or FAQs help with that.

Example Prompts:

- "Create a blog post outline with headings, subheadings, and bullet points on how to hire your first virtual assistant."
- "Write a LinkedIn article that includes an introduction, three main points, a summary, and a call to action."
- "Format this blog post using numbered steps and include a conclusion with key takeaways."

By using prompts like these, you not only make the most of AI writing tools, but you also generate content that is easier for language models to read, understand, and recommend. The structure, tone, and clarity of your content matter just as much as the information itself. The better your prompt, the more aligned your content will be with how AI tools search, interpret, and serve information to users.

Prompt design is the new starting point for influence in the AI era. Learn to master it, and your message will reach further than ever before.

Monitoring your brand mentions across AI tools

As AI tools like ChatGPT, Claude, Gemini, and Perplexity.ai become the new way people search for information, it is more important than ever to monitor how your brand is being mentioned across these platforms. Just as you would track brand visibility in traditional search engines or on social media, you now need to understand how AI models are referencing your business, your content, and your reputation. This is a critical step in maintaining relevance, improving trust, and staying competitive in an AI-first digital landscape.

Monitoring your brand mentions in AI tools helps you answer an essential question: when people ask for recommendations or insights, is your brand part of the conversation? If not, you need to find out why. And if it is, you want to know how you are being represented, what tone is being used, and whether the information is accurate and helpful.

One of the first things to do is test how these AI platforms respond to prompts related to your industry or service. Ask ChatGPT, "What are the top business coaching communities?" or "Who offers mindset training for entrepreneurs?" If your brand does not come up, that is a signal that your content or digital footprint might not be strong enough in the places these models are drawing from. This kind of testing can help you identify gaps and guide your content strategy moving forward.

Another approach is to use tools that track mentions across public platforms known to be indexed by AI models. Platforms like Reddit, Quora, LinkedIn, and Medium are regularly used by large language models for training and reference. Monitoring brand mentions in these spaces will give you insight into how people talk about your business, whether your contributions are gaining traction, and what reputation signals might be feeding into AI responses.

You can set up Google Alerts for your brand name, website URL, and key offerings. While Google Alerts was designed for tracking search results and news articles, it can still catch new mentions in forums and blog posts that AI tools may eventually use. Tools like Mention, Brand24, and Talkwalker offer more advanced monitoring features and can help you track sentiment, keyword trends, and emerging mentions in real time. These platforms are especially useful if your brand operates in multiple markets or languages.

Also, pay attention to how your content performs on your own platforms. If you are publishing on YouTube, Substack, a blog, or a podcast, track which pieces are getting linked to, shared, or quoted. AI models prioritize content that has visibility, credibility, and consistent messaging across different platforms. The more your content is engaged with and referenced online, the more likely it is that AI tools will identify it as a reliable source.

Reviewing how your business appears in local directories and review sites is another key step. Make sure your profiles on Google My Business, Yelp, and Trustpilot are accurate and active. AI models often pull from these sites when asked for service-based recommendations. Encourage satisfied clients to leave detailed reviews that describe what made their experience with you valuable. This not only helps with reputation management but also gives AI models the kind of natural language feedback they can incorporate into future responses.

When possible, contribute to discussions in AI-visible forums. Answer questions on Quora, share insights on LinkedIn, and participate in relevant Reddit threads. These interactions increase your visibility and demonstrate authority. Many AI models use a mixture of user-generated content and expert articles to form their answers. Showing up in both categories helps reinforce your brand presence from multiple angles.

You should also check how your competitors are being mentioned. If you ask an AI model for the best service providers in your niche and your competitors are listed but you are not, study what digital signals they may be sending. Are they featured in a high-ranking Medium article? Do they have a Wikipedia page? Are they getting quoted on industry blogs or included in well-reviewed directories? Use this research to refine your strategy and identify areas where you can increase your digital visibility.

Finally, make monitoring an ongoing process. Set aside time each month to check how AI tools talk about your industry and whether your brand is appearing in the responses. Review your digital presence across major platforms, keep track of what content is ranking well, and adjust your publishing efforts based on the data. As AI models continue to evolve, your visibility within them will depend on your ability to stay engaged, stay consistent, and stay strategic.

Monitoring brand mentions in AI tools is not just about recognition. It is about understanding your place in the future of search and recommendation. By keeping a close eye on where and how your brand appears in AI outputs, you gain the insights you need to guide your marketing, improve your content, and position your business as a go-to resource in your field.

8

Chapter 8: Creating Your Own AI Entity

Building a GPT or assistant based on your business

Creating your own GPT or AI assistant based on your business is one of the smartest ways to establish a powerful presence in the AI-driven economy. Instead of waiting to be discovered by other AI platforms, you can take control by building a custom assistant that knows your business, speaks in your voice, and delivers expert-level answers to your customers. Whether you want to improve customer service, increase lead generation, or automate parts of your sales process, a tailored assistant gives your business a unique edge.

At its core, building a GPT or assistant means training or configuring an AI model to understand your content, your tone, and your specific offerings. This assistant can then interact with users through your website, social media, or internal tools, delivering personalized and consistent responses that reflect your brand values.

To begin, you need to clarify the purpose of your assistant. Ask yourself what problems it should solve for your business. Do you want it to answer frequently asked questions about your services? Guide users through your programs? Help new visitors find the right resource or product? Or perhaps you want it to onboard new clients, help team members get up to speed, or even assist with internal training? Starting with a clear goal helps you build a focused assistant that delivers real value.

Once your objective is defined, gather your content. This includes website copy, blog posts, product descriptions, service pages, case studies, FAQs, and any guides or frameworks you have developed. You want the assistant to reflect your actual knowledge and processes, not just generic responses. Think of this content as the training material that will shape how your assistant communicates and what it can help users accomplish.

Next, choose the platform for building your assistant. OpenAI's GPT Builder is a user-friendly option if you want to create a custom GPT model quickly. Other tools like Zapier's AI integrations, Botpress, Voiceflow, and custom APIs can also help you deploy your assistant across web and mobile apps. Some platforms allow you to upload documents or link to URLs so the AI can learn directly from your material. This is useful if you already have content you want the assistant to reference without having to retype or reformat it.

When building the assistant, pay close attention to how you define its personality and tone. This is where your brand voice comes into play. Make it sound like you. If your brand is warm and conversational, train the assistant to use everyday language and speak with clarity. If you want it to sound authoritative and professional, provide examples of how you communicate in emails, proposals, or coaching sessions. The more you guide its style, the more it will sound like an extension of your brand.

You should also build in the ability for the assistant to handle common scenarios. Think about the top 10 questions your customers ask. These should be programmed in as key conversation paths. You can include fallback answers and links to additional resources, so the assistant never reaches a dead end. If possible, build a system for feedback so users can rate their experience and help you refine the assistant over time.

Integration is the next step. A GPT assistant is only useful if it is accessible to your audience. Add it to your website, especially on service pages, blog posts, and contact forms. Consider deploying it in your client portal, your community platform, or even in your email marketing system as a way to engage subscribers in two-way conversations. If your business has a mobile app, embedding the assistant there makes your content available around the clock in a format that feels like a personal concierge.

You can also use the assistant as a lead generation tool. When someone asks a question, the assistant can respond with value and then prompt the user to join your email list, book a consultation, or register for an event. Because the interaction feels natural and helpful, users are more likely to convert. Over time, this creates a flywheel of value where every visitor has the chance to interact meaningfully with your business, even when you are not available in person.

For internal use, a GPT-based assistant can serve as a training guide for new team members, a quick-access knowledge base, or a decision-support tool for your sales team. By organizing your internal processes and documentation into AI-ready formats, your assistant becomes a central hub for how your business runs. This reduces repetitive training, improves consistency, and empowers your team to move faster with more confidence.

Security and privacy should also be considered. If your assistant handles sensitive data or interacts with customer information, make sure the platform you choose complies with relevant regulations and follows strong data protection standards. You may need to limit what data the assistant can access or provide transparency about how user interactions are handled.

Once your assistant is live, continue to optimize it. Track how people use it. Look at which questions come up most often and which responses get the best feedback. Update the knowledge base regularly with new content, offers, and case studies. Your business evolves, and your assistant should evolve with it.

In a world where AI is becoming the first place people go for answers, building your own GPT-based assistant is like launching a digital version of your expertise. It scales your voice, shares your knowledge, and gives every visitor a personalized experience. And best of all, it keeps working for you even when you are asleep, in a meeting, or focused on your next big project. This is not just about automation. It is about creating a smart, scalable presence that makes your brand more responsive, more visible, and more competitive.

Training your GPT on your knowledge base, FAQs, and unique frameworks

Training your GPT on your own knowledge base, FAQs, and unique frameworks is one of the most effective ways to create a smart assistant that truly represents your business. While many AI tools are powerful right out of the box, they become significantly more valuable when you tailor them with the content, language, and systems specific to your brand. This turns your GPT into more than just a chatbot. It becomes a digital extension of your expertise that can respond with accuracy, personality, and clarity.

To start, gather your foundational content. This includes the material you have already created to explain your services, products, values, and customer process. Your knowledge base might include articles, guides, email responses, customer onboarding documents, and any internal documentation you have developed over time. Include case studies, testimonials, and the way you usually answer client questions. If you have a team, think about the emails they send, the checklists they use, and the materials they share with customers. All of that represents your operational knowledge and can be used to build a more intelligent assistant.

Next, organize your FAQs. These are the most common questions people ask about your business. Whether it is about pricing, timelines, how your process works, or what kind of results you deliver, these questions give you a window into what matters to your audience. Write out clear, detailed answers in your own voice. When training your GPT, this content serves as your foundation for customer-facing communication. If you already have an FAQ page on your website, use that as a starting point. You can expand it with answers from past emails, consultations, and social media replies. The more real examples you include, the more naturally your assistant will respond.

If you have developed a signature framework, methodology, or system, this is where your assistant can really stand out. Frameworks are what make your business unique. Whether it is a five-step process you use to coach clients or a content creation system you teach in workshops, these frameworks are essential to train into your GPT. Start by writing out your process in detail. Break it down step by step. Explain what each stage means, why it matters, and how it helps the user. Give your assistant access to this structure so it can confidently walk people through your proprietary approach.

Once you have your content prepared, use a tool that allows you to upload or link your documents directly. Many GPT builders and AI platforms now support document training, where you can teach the assistant by feeding it

PDFs, URLs, or structured text. If the platform supports knowledge retrieval, make sure the assistant can look up answers from your uploaded material during a conversation. This gives your GPT the ability to reference your knowledge without making things up, resulting in higher accuracy and more trust with users.

Structure your content in a way that makes it easy for the AI to understand. Use clear headings, bullet points, and labeled sections. For example, label a section as "Step 1: Define Your Audience" if you are teaching a marketing process. Avoid using vague or overly creative titles. Language models work best when the content is straightforward and logically organized. You can still inject personality into your examples and tone, but the formatting should help the AI quickly locate and use the right information.

When testing your assistant, simulate real user interactions. Ask the GPT common questions you receive and evaluate the responses. See if it can correctly explain your process, answer objections, and guide a new user. If it struggles or provides incomplete answers, go back and refine your source material. Often, gaps in performance are tied to missing context or unclear explanations in the training content.

Keep in mind that training your GPT is not a one-time task. Your business evolves, and so should your assistant. Make it a habit to update your knowledge base regularly. When you create a new service, develop a new framework, or publish new content, train your assistant with those updates. This ensures it stays current and aligned with your latest messaging.

You should also create fallback answers for when your assistant cannot provide an exact response. These answers can direct users to book a call, fill out a contact form, or check a particular page on your website. This keeps the user journey moving forward and avoids the frustration that can come from a dead-end response.

Training your GPT on your knowledge base, FAQs, and unique frameworks empowers your business in three big ways. First, it creates a consistent and personalized customer experience at scale. Second, it reinforces your brand authority by sharing your exact processes and voice. And third, it positions you ahead of competitors who still rely on generic automation tools.

In a world where AI is shaping how people interact with brands, the businesses that take time to train their own assistant will stand out as leaders. Your GPT becomes your twenty-four-hour coach, guide, and representative. And when it speaks your language and teaches your unique method, it becomes a true asset in growing your brand and building trust with every interaction.

Use cases for lead generation, customer service, and brand authority

Artificial intelligence is changing how businesses attract, engage, and serve their audiences. When used with purpose, AI can help you grow your business by generating leads, improving customer service, and building brand authority. These three use cases are essential to staying competitive and visible in a market where AI tools are now at the front line of user interaction. By understanding how to apply AI in these areas, you create new pathways for growth while increasing your efficiency and reach.

Lead Generation

AI is one of the most powerful tools available for lead generation. Instead of relying solely on forms or cold outreach, you can use AI to interact with prospects in real time, guide them to the right solution, and capture their information at the exact moment they show interest. For example, a custom GPT or AI assistant on your website can answer questions, explain your services, and offer next steps such as booking a call or downloading a free resource. Because the assistant speaks in your voice and uses your content, it feels like a natural extension of you.

Another approach is using AI to qualify leads. Rather than having your team spend hours chasing down bad fits, an AI tool can ask a few smart questions, determine if the person is your ideal customer, and route them appropriately. If they are a good fit, they are invited to schedule a discovery call. If they are not ready yet, the assistant can guide them to your blog, email list, or video library until they are warmed up.

AI can also help you personalize your lead magnets and follow-ups. With the right prompts, you can create ebooks, reports, or assessments tailored to specific industries or pain points. When someone downloads a resource, AI tools can send personalized emails based on the user's interests, increasing open rates and conversions. You are no longer sending the same message to everyone. Instead, your lead generation system becomes responsive, helpful, and targeted.

Customer Service

Customer service is often the first impression someone has with your business. AI makes it possible to deliver fast, helpful, and consistent support even when your team is offline or overwhelmed. A trained assistant can answer frequently asked questions, handle basic requests, and provide step-by-step support using your knowledge base. This frees up your team to focus on higher-level interactions while ensuring no customer is left waiting for help.

For example, imagine a customer visiting your website late at night with a question about your refund policy or how to access a course they purchased. Instead of sending an email and waiting until morning, they get an immediate response from your assistant. It walks them through the process, links them to the right page, and even updates their account information if needed. That kind of service builds trust and keeps customers engaged.

AI can also track common customer issues and alert you to patterns. If a large number of users are asking about a specific feature or experiencing confusion with a certain step, your assistant can flag that. This gives you the chance to update your instructions, fix bugs, or create better documentation. Over time, your service improves, and your customers feel more supported.

For coaching businesses, AI can also offer supplemental guidance. If a client has a question between sessions, the assistant can refer them to your frameworks, worksheets, or past content. This keeps the coaching process moving without always requiring a direct call or message. It is like giving every client their own personal guide based on your teaching style and resources.

Brand Authority

Being visible in AI-generated answers is the new frontier of authority. AI is already shaping how people search, learn, and make decisions. When your content, voice, and expertise are represented accurately by AI tools, your brand gains credibility. People begin to associate you with specific insights, processes, and solutions.

One of the best ways to build brand authority is by using AI to create and distribute high-quality content. You can use AI to write blog posts, create scripts for YouTube videos, generate LinkedIn articles, and develop lead magnets that showcase your knowledge. The more consistent and valuable your content is, the more AI tools will begin to recognize your name, reference your materials, and rank your work.

Another powerful use case is training your own GPT assistant to explain your unique frameworks and methods. When someone interacts with your assistant and gets helpful, expert-level answers, they immediately see you as a trusted guide. The assistant reflects your knowledge, your systems, and your style. Over time, this becomes a direct channel to build familiarity and trust with both prospects and current clients.

You can also use AI to repurpose your content into formats that match different learning styles. Turn blog posts into podcast outlines, summarize webinars into newsletters, or break long-form content into short social media posts. The more touchpoints you create, the more your brand stays top of mind. AI makes this efficient and scalable without sacrificing quality.

In a crowded market, authority is about more than just having a good product or service. It is about being present in the right conversations, offering real value, and showing up with consistency. AI helps you do all three. From generating leads to delivering world-class support to positioning you as an expert, AI is no longer just a tool. It is a strategic advantage for business owners who are ready to lead in the new digital economy.

9

Chapter 9: Tracking & Measuring AIO Success

What metrics to track (mentions in AI outputs, traffic from AI-integrated platforms, branded search)

To know whether your AI Optimization strategy is working, you need to track the right metrics. These indicators show if your brand is gaining visibility across AI platforms and if users are actually finding and engaging with your content through those tools. Just like with SEO, where you monitor rankings, backlinks, and traffic, AIO requires a new lens. The focus is on how well your brand performs in AI-driven environments where traditional analytics tools may not capture the full picture.

Mentions in AI Outputs

One of the most valuable metrics to track is how often your brand is being mentioned by AI tools like ChatGPT, Claude, Perplexity, and Gemini. These tools are becoming the new default for search, and showing up in their answers is a strong signal that your content is being recognized as credible and useful. You can test this manually by asking relevant questions and seeing whether your brand appears. For example, ask a tool, "What are the best business coaching platforms for entrepreneurs?" or "What is a good mindset program for business owners?" If your name or brand is mentioned in the response, that is a sign you are on the right track.

You can also monitor forums and public platforms that AI tools pull from. Check Reddit, Quora, Medium, YouTube transcripts, and blogs where your content or name is mentioned. These platforms are often used in AI training data, so the more your brand is discussed in these spaces, the more likely you will be included in future AI responses.

Traffic from AI-Integrated Platforms

Another key metric is traffic coming from platforms that integrate AI into their user experience. While it may not always be obvious when traffic is generated by AI suggestions, you can watch for upticks in visits following major content uploads or activity on AI-visible platforms. For example, if you publish a detailed answer on Quora or Reddit and suddenly see a spike in site traffic, that content may have been pulled into an AI-generated response and prompted users to visit your page.

Look closely at referral traffic in your analytics tool. If you start receiving visits from sources like Perplexity.ai or links posted in LinkedIn articles, newsletters, or Medium posts that were likely surfaced by AI tools, that is a sign your visibility is growing. You can also track embedded widgets, chatbot traffic, and the click-through rates from AI-powered interfaces you control, such as your own website assistant or knowledge bot.

For podcasts and YouTube, track how often transcripts are downloaded or cited. These platforms are increasingly scraped and referenced by LLMs, so any content that performs well there could lead to increased visibility inside AI systems, especially those trained on spoken-word or long-form text.

Branded Search

Branded search is another reliable indicator that your AI Optimization is working. If more people begin searching for your name, business, or products specifically, it means that awareness is increasing. Often, users who discover a name through an AI recommendation will follow up with a search to learn more. If your branded search traffic grows after you start producing optimized content and engaging in AI-friendly platforms, it is a clear sign your strategy is paying off.

Tools like Google Search Console and analytics platforms like Ahrefs or SEMrush can help you monitor branded search volume. Pay attention to keyword variations as well. If you notice people searching for terms like "Michael Wilson business coach" or "Entrepreneur Power Network community," it shows that your content and authority are reaching new audiences.

You can also use branded search insights to discover what people want to know about you. Look at the questions being asked alongside your name. Are they looking for your services, testimonials, or how to contact you? This gives you guidance on what to publish next and how to refine your assistant or website to answer those questions directly.

Engagement Metrics

Visibility is important, but so is engagement. Monitor how users interact with your AI-driven experiences. Track how many people use your GPT assistant, how long they stay engaged, what kind of questions they ask, and whether they take action afterward. High engagement indicates that your assistant is providing value and creating meaningful experiences for your audience.

If you are using AI to write content, pay attention to the performance of those pieces. Measure views, time on page, shares, and bounce rates. If content created or optimized for AI platforms performs better than other content, you know you are on the right path.

Also, keep track of conversion-related metrics. Are AI-driven interactions leading to more newsletter signups, consultation bookings, or product sales? The true value of AIO comes from turning visibility into results. By tying user activity back to business outcomes, you can demonstrate a clear return on investment for your AI strategy.

Summary

Tracking mentions in AI outputs, traffic from AI-integrated platforms, and branded search volume gives you a clear view of how well your brand is performing in this new AI-first landscape. These are the signals that tell you whether your voice is being heard, your content is being used, and your business is gaining authority. Combine these metrics with strong engagement and conversion data, and you will have everything you need to fine-tune your AIO efforts and continue growing your presence in the age of artificial intelligence.

Tools and dashboards

As AI Optimization becomes more important for business visibility, having the right tools and dashboards in place is critical. These platforms help you measure your reach, manage your content, track mentions across AI-indexed sources, and fine-tune your strategy over time. Just like SEO tools gave businesses insight into how they ranked on Google, AIO tools give you a window into how AI platforms are interacting with your brand.

Content Management and Optimization Tools

Frase and **Surfer SEO** are excellent tools that help you optimize your content for semantic relevance, structure, and clarity. These tools were originally built for traditional SEO but now play a key role in formatting content for AI consumption. They help you identify related keywords, answer intent-based questions, and ensure your content is digestible for both humans and machines.

Jasper and **Writesonic** are content-generation platforms powered by AI that can help you draft blog posts, emails, and web pages that match the tone and clarity needed for AIO. You can train these tools on your brand voice, use them to create outlines, and generate content specifically designed to be understood and trusted by large language models.

Mention and Brand Tracking Tools

Brand24, **Mention**, and **Talkwalker** are monitoring tools that track your brand mentions across the internet. These are especially useful for keeping an eye on forums, blogs, and review platforms that AI tools frequently crawl. You can set alerts for your name, company, domain, or keywords related to your services. These tools also help you track sentiment, so you can understand how your brand is being perceived across platforms that influence AI training and responses.

AI-Specific Platforms and Assistants

OpenAI's Custom GPTs allow you to build and train your own assistant using your content, tone, and FAQs. This gives you the ability to provide consistent, on-brand interactions across your site, community, or internal systems. It can also serve as a lead generation or support tool, helping users find the right resources while giving you insight into what questions are most common.

Perplexity.ai is both a research tool and a window into how AI may pull in real-time web content. It shows citations and sources behind its answers, which gives you clues about what types of content are surfacing most often and how to structure your own materials to get included.

Analytics Dashboards

For performance tracking, you can use **Google Analytics** and **Google Search Console** to monitor branded search traffic, referral sources, and user behavior across your site. These tools help you identify where users are coming from and which pages are performing best.

In addition, **Microsoft Clarity** and **Hotjar** give you behavioral insights, such as how users interact with your content, where they scroll, and when they drop off. These tools are especially useful for improving the user experience on AI-driven landing pages and assistant-enabled sites.

If you have an AI assistant deployed on your site, many platforms offer built-in analytics. Look for data on user interactions, popular questions, bounce rates, and conversion triggers. This information helps you refine the assistant's knowledge and improve its ability to engage with users.

Workflow and Content Distribution

To manage publishing across channels that feed into AI models, tools like **Buffer**, **Hootsuite**, or **Later** can help you schedule content consistently across platforms like LinkedIn, Medium, YouTube, and Reddit. AI often references these platforms, so maintaining regular, high-quality publishing activity increases your chances of being cited.

Zapier or **Make (Integromat)** can be used to automate your workflows, such as sending new blog posts to your assistant for training, reposting content to forums, or tracking keywords that appear in Reddit or Quora discussions.

Custom Dashboards

If you want a centralized view of your AIO performance, you can build a custom dashboard using tools like **Google Data Studio** or **Notion**. These can pull in metrics from multiple sources, such as brand mentions, traffic data, user interactions, and assistant feedback. A unified dashboard helps you make informed decisions and spot patterns over time.

The tools and dashboards you choose will depend on your goals, but the objective remains the same: understand how AI tools are interacting with your brand and use that insight to stay visible, valuable, and trustworthy. By combining content optimization platforms, monitoring tools, assistant analytics, and data dashboards, you create an AIO system that not only measures success but continuously improves it. This is the new frontier of business intelligence, and the sooner you set it up, the stronger your competitive edge will be.

How to ask ChatGPT or other LLMs questions to test your visibility

One of the simplest and most effective ways to gauge how visible your business is to AI platforms is by asking them direct, strategic questions. Tools like ChatGPT, Claude, and Gemini are designed to provide relevant answers based on what they have learned from online content. When you ask questions related to your industry, niche, or expertise, you can see whether your brand, name, or content shows up in the response. This is a practical method for testing how well your AI Optimization efforts are working.

Start by thinking like your ideal customer. What would someone ask an AI if they were looking for a solution you provide? Formulate natural, question-based prompts that reflect how users interact with these platforms. Instead of asking, "Who is Michael Wilson?" try something like, "Who are the top business coaches helping entrepreneurs grow their networks?" or "What are some trusted communities for business owners who want to learn about automation?" These types of questions are what real users type or speak, and they are also what trigger the AI to scan for sources it trusts.

Vary the type of questions you ask. Try informational queries like, "What is AIO and how is it different from SEO?" as well as transactional prompts such as, "Where can I find a course that teaches AI-powered book writing for entrepreneurs?" You can also test authority-focused prompts like, "What frameworks are used by experts to help business owners scale with AI?" or "Which communities focus on helping solopreneurs build their online presence?" Each of these variations will reveal how the AI perceives your digital footprint and whether your content is indexed, trusted, and relevant.

Make sure to test these prompts across multiple platforms. ChatGPT and Claude may draw from slightly different training data, while tools like Perplexity.ai often include real-time web sources with citations. When you use Perplexity, look for the actual sources it references. If you see your site, blog, LinkedIn posts, or mentions in public forums being cited, that is a strong indicator that your content is feeding into AI-generated answers. It also tells you which pieces of content are performing well from an AIO perspective.

Track your results over time. Create a list of test prompts and revisit them monthly to see if your visibility improves. If your business name begins to appear in answers that it was previously excluded from, it suggests that your AIO content strategy is starting to gain traction. If your name never appears, even after publishing on AI-friendly platforms and optimizing your content, that may indicate a need to refine your messaging, increase your content volume, or pursue more high-authority placements.

Another approach is to ask LLMs about topics you know you have written about. If you published a guide on business automation or hosted a podcast episode on building community through AI, ask questions that should point to that content. If the AI does not reference it, consider whether the piece is well structured, accessible, and posted on platforms that AI tools recognize. You may need to revise how it is formatted, repost it on higher-traffic platforms, or add more internal links that make it easier for AI to interpret the context.

You can also explore how your competitors show up in AI responses. Ask questions that are relevant to your industry and see which names and brands are consistently mentioned. Analyze what kind of content they produce, where they publish it, and how it is structured. This gives you a model to benchmark against and ideas for how to position your own business to increase visibility.

Use these prompts not just to test your exposure but to guide your strategy. The responses you receive can reveal what the AI is prioritizing. If tools favor list-style content, expert tips, or community-focused platforms, that is a signal to adjust your own output in that direction. Over time, the more your name appears in relevant answers, the stronger your authority becomes in the eyes of both AI platforms and the users who rely on them.

How to collect feedback from AI-powered searchers

As more users rely on AI platforms to discover solutions, businesses must adapt not only by being visible in these tools but also by learning from the people who find them through this channel. Collecting feedback from AI-powered searchers gives you insights into what information users are seeking, how well your content answers their questions, and what adjustments can help you serve them better. This feedback becomes the fuel that drives stronger engagement, trust, and conversion in a world where AI influences discovery.

Begin by asking your audience how they found you. Add a simple question to your intake forms, surveys, or email sign-ups that asks, "Did you find us through an AI tool like ChatGPT, Claude, or Perplexity?" You can offer multiple-choice options that include search engines, referrals, social media, and AI platforms. This gives you clear data on how many of your new leads are arriving through AI-generated recommendations. Over time, patterns will emerge that help you understand where to focus your optimization efforts.

You can also add feedback forms directly to the content that AI tools are likely to surface. On blog posts, YouTube video descriptions, or landing pages, place a short form that asks visitors whether they found the content helpful or if something was missing. Include a field that allows them to mention how they discovered the page. This allows you to connect the dots between AI visibility and actual user behavior. Keep the form simple to encourage responses without interrupting the user experience.

Another way to gather insight is by engaging your community. If you have an online group, email list, or social following, ask your audience whether they use AI tools to search for information and how often they do. Encourage them to share examples of what they asked and what kind of answers they received. This qualitative feedback shows you how your target market interacts with AI and what kind of language or content structure gets their attention. It also helps you tailor your content to align with the phrasing and style users are already accustomed to.

For those using a custom GPT or AI assistant on their site, review conversation logs or interaction summaries. These logs often reveal the exact questions users ask and where they drop off. If someone asks a question and receives an incomplete or confusing answer, that is a signal to improve your training materials or restructure your knowledge base. If users consistently ask about a specific product or service, that indicates strong demand and may lead to better conversions if you enhance that part of your content.

Use automated tools to monitor AI-related engagement as well. Services like Hotjar and Microsoft Clarity allow you to watch how users behave on pages optimized for AI visibility. Track where they click, how long they stay, and whether they engage with lead magnets or support tools. If a blog post receives sudden traffic spikes and users are staying longer, it may have been mentioned or linked to by an AI tool. Compare this behavioral data with your publishing calendar to see what kind of content gets the strongest response.

Email follow-ups are another effective method. When someone opts into your list or downloads a resource, include a quick question in your welcome sequence asking where they heard about you. Phrase it casually, such as, "Did a friend refer you, or did you find us through an AI tool like ChatGPT?" This not only gathers useful data but also opens the door to a conversation about what they were looking for and whether your material delivered.

If you notice that certain AI-generated responses bring in more leads, study the language and formatting used in those pieces. Then, apply the same structure to other areas of your site or content. Use follow-up surveys to ask whether the information matched what the user was hoping to find, and invite suggestions on how to improve clarity, depth, or usability.

Collecting feedback from AI-powered searchers gives you a competitive edge. These users are often more intentional, seeking solutions with a clear goal in mind. By tracking how they arrive, what they engage with, and how they respond, you gain the ability to refine your messaging and serve them more effectively. The more you listen to their input, the better your AI Optimization strategy becomes.

10

Chapter 10: Future-Proofing Your Business in the AI Era

What's coming next in AI search and visibility

The landscape of search is evolving quickly, and AI is at the center of that transformation. Traditional search engines are being replaced by conversational interfaces powered by large language models. These tools are becoming the first stop for information discovery, decision-making, and recommendations. As the technology continues to improve, visibility strategies must adapt. Businesses that stay ahead of these changes will benefit from early authority and sustained attention, while others may fall behind.

One of the most significant shifts coming is the integration of real-time, multimodal inputs. AI tools are beginning to process not just text but also images, video, audio, and live data. This means content strategies must expand beyond blog posts and articles. Businesses will need to optimize YouTube channels, podcast transcripts, infographics, and even product photos to ensure their information is accessible to these advanced models. When someone asks a question that requires visual or auditory context, the AI will pull from those formats just as easily as it does from text.

Another major development is the personalization of AI responses. As users interact more with AI tools, these systems learn preferences, past behavior, and intent patterns. Search results are becoming custom-tailored to the individual. This means that your content not only needs to be accurate and useful but also adaptable to different audiences. Businesses that create layered content for beginners, intermediates, and advanced users will be more likely to appear across a range of user profiles.

Expect to see more integration between AI tools and e-commerce or service platforms. Users will not just get recommendations, they will be able to complete transactions directly from within AI interfaces. This creates an opportunity for businesses to build in transactional capabilities into their AI-optimized content. Calls to action like booking a call, purchasing a product, or accessing a course will become part of the natural flow of an AI conversation. Your content will need to anticipate these moments and support them with structured responses and links.

AI models are also moving toward citation and sourcing transparency. This means that tools will increasingly show where information came from and who the original source is. Businesses that build content on trusted platforms and contribute to widely referenced sources will have a better chance of being cited. Platforms like Medium, Quora, Reddit, and LinkedIn are already showing signs of being used as preferred data sources. Getting active on these channels with high-quality content will play a larger role in your visibility strategy.

Voice interfaces are expected to grow rapidly. As smart assistants and devices become more common, people will ask questions aloud and expect quick, relevant answers. Optimizing your content for voice-based interactions will require simple phrasing, clear structure, and natural language. Short sentences, direct answers, and clarity of intent will be crucial in making sure your business shows up when users speak rather than type.

AI-generated summaries and answers are being embedded across tools people use every day, from email platforms and browsers to customer service dashboards and productivity apps. This wide distribution of AI-generated content means that your visibility must extend beyond search engines and websites. Your brand and message need to be present in the underlying data these tools pull from. Syndicating your insights across multiple platforms, maintaining a strong digital footprint, and consistently updating your knowledge base will help you stay visible in these distributed

AI environments.

Another trend to watch is the rise of proprietary AI ecosystems. Companies like OpenAI, Google, Meta, and Amazon are each developing their own AI platforms with unique behaviors, preferences, and data access. Businesses will need to optimize content for multiple ecosystems, not just one. What works in ChatGPT may differ from what gets attention in Gemini or Meta AI. Staying flexible and paying attention to performance across different models will become a vital skill for marketers and business owners.

AI compliance and regulation will also influence visibility. As governments introduce standards around bias, accuracy, and data usage, the content that gets surfaced by AI tools may be filtered based on trust and authority ratings. Businesses that focus on transparency, ethical messaging, and verifiable claims will have a better chance of being favored by algorithms that prioritize safe and accurate responses.

The future of AI search and visibility is not about gaming the system or chasing algorithms. It is about building meaningful content, structured for discovery, that genuinely helps people. As AI continues to shape how information is found and trusted, business owners must be proactive, adaptable, and intentional. The next phase of visibility will be earned by those who understand the behavior of these tools, speak the language of their audience, and consistently show up where AI looks for answers.

Preparing for personalized AI agents and assistant-based browsing

The next wave of digital interaction is shifting toward personalized AI agents and assistant-based browsing. These tools are designed to anticipate user needs, provide answers before a formal query is made, and guide individuals through decision-making processes in real time. Rather than relying on static web searches, users will increasingly depend on AI assistants that act as proactive digital concierges. This transformation changes how businesses must position themselves to remain visible and valuable in a world where the AI does the browsing on behalf of the user.

Personalized AI agents will be trained on an individual's behavior, preferences, and previous interactions. This means the answers people receive will vary based on their unique profile, making visibility less about ranking for one-size-fits-all keywords and more about context, relevance, and trustworthiness. To prepare, your content must serve different customer journeys and provide layered responses that match varying levels of knowledge, urgency, and interest.

The structure and tone of your content must be easy for AI to digest, summarize, and prioritize. These agents are trained to identify helpful, clear, and structured content that aligns with user intent. Long, vague pages or poorly organized resources will be ignored in favor of concise, authoritative sources. You will need to optimize your site architecture, content formatting, and metadata to ensure that your information is easy to navigate not just for humans but for AI systems that are parsing content on the user's behalf.

Assistant-based browsing means that users will no longer need to click through multiple links or sift through a list of search results. Instead, AI assistants will aggregate, compare, and recommend options. This puts a premium on content that is accurate, current, and easily referenced. Keeping your information updated, well-sourced, and aligned with common user questions will help AI assistants select your business as a trusted option. Focus on clearly stating what you do, who you serve, and how users can take action, whether that is booking a call, accessing a resource, or purchasing a product.

Another key consideration is interoperability. Personalized AI agents will operate across platforms and devices, pulling data from calendars, emails, browsing habits, and voice commands. If your content and services are not integrated into these systems, you may be left out of the conversation. Businesses that develop APIs, voice-compatible tools, or assistant-ready landing pages will gain a strategic advantage. For example, having a chatbot trained on your knowledge base that can integrate with popular assistants like Alexa or Google Assistant will increase your reach and responsiveness.

Trust will become one of the most important factors in AI assistant recommendations. If a tool is choosing options on behalf of a user, it will favor businesses with a strong reputation, transparent policies, and social proof. Encourage reviews, testimonials, and third-party references across platforms like Trustpilot, LinkedIn, and Reddit. These signals will be read by AI tools as proof that your business delivers on its promises. The more consistently your brand is seen as reliable and high quality, the more likely it is to be included in recommendations from personalized agents.

Preparing for this future also involves training your own assistant. Building a custom GPT or branded AI helper ensures that your audience can engage with your expertise directly, on your terms. You can use these assistants to onboard new leads, provide support, and walk customers through complex decisions. As assistant-based browsing becomes the norm, your custom tools will help users navigate your offerings more efficiently while reinforcing your brand authority.

The shift to personalized AI agents and assistant-based browsing is not just a change in technology. It is a change in how trust is earned, how attention is allocated, and how decisions are made. By designing your content, tools, and customer journey around these emerging patterns, you position your business to stay visible and competitive in the new digital landscape.

Building a business that thrives in the AI-first world

To build a business that thrives in an AI-first world, you need to shift your mindset from being found through traditional search to being understood, trusted, and recommended by intelligent systems. Visibility now means more than ranking at the top of a search engine. It means being woven into the answers, conversations, and decision-making processes that AI tools guide every day. Thriving in this new environment requires strategic positioning, adaptable content, and a brand presence that communicates clarity and authority at every touchpoint.

Start by understanding how your audience is using AI. Customers are no longer simply searching. They are conversing with tools like ChatGPT, Claude, Gemini, and others. These tools provide direct answers, summarize insights, and make suggestions based on vast pools of data. Your business needs to exist within those pools in a meaningful way. That means creating content that aligns with natural language questions, offering solutions in a structured format, and distributing your knowledge across the platforms these tools are trained on.

Your messaging must be crystal clear. AI systems rely on clarity to interpret intent and match user queries with accurate information. Avoid vague descriptions of what you do. Instead, define your services, explain your process, and use the language your customers use when they are seeking help. The more specific and well-structured your content is, the more likely it will be surfaced in AI-generated responses.

Consistency across all platforms is critical. AI tools pull from multiple sources to build a picture of your brand. Your website, social media, videos, podcasts, and even comments on forums contribute to how AI understands and represents you. A business that thrives in this environment maintains a cohesive message, voice, and tone regardless of the platform. This means your About page, LinkedIn bio, podcast intro, and Medium articles all need to tell the same story and point toward the same value.

You also need to create systems that allow you to scale your content and engagement without adding unnecessary complexity. Use AI to your advantage by automating routine tasks, generating outlines, summarizing long-form content, and testing new ideas. Train your own assistant or GPT to handle frequently asked questions, lead qualification, or onboarding. These tools do not replace human connection but enhance your ability to deliver it at scale.

Invest in your digital footprint. That means contributing to platforms where AI tools gather their training data. Write for Medium, post value-driven answers on Quora and Reddit, and create video content for YouTube. Participate in podcasts, publish transcripts, and gather reviews on trusted third-party sites. These assets help AI validate your authority and surface your name more often in relevant discussions.

Anticipate user needs. A business that thrives in an AI-first world understands its audience deeply and creates content that addresses real problems. Think beyond marketing and focus on education, clarity, and usefulness. The more your content helps people understand, decide, and take action, the more value AI tools will assign to it.

Finally, stay agile. The world of AI is evolving quickly, and strategies that work today may shift tomorrow. Monitor how AI tools mention your brand, track what types of content get surfaced, and adapt your approach based on feedback. Continue testing, learning, and refining your digital presence so your business remains part of the conversation no matter how the tools change.

Thriving in an AI-first world is about relevance, reliability, and readiness. It is not about chasing algorithms. It is about building a business that is easy to understand, trusted by both machines and humans, and designed to deliver value in every interaction. When your business becomes part of the way AI tools explain the world, you create a competitive edge that lasts.

11

AIO checklist

AIO Content Strategy

- Identify your ideal audience's most common questions
- Create long-form, evergreen content that answers real user intent
- Use natural, conversational language aligned with how people ask questions
- Incorporate summaries and key takeaways at the top and bottom of each piece
- Add FAQs using real queries from platforms like Reddit, Quora, or search autocomplete

✅ **Content Formatting for AI Comprehension**

- Structure content using clear headings (H1, H2, H3)
- Use bullet points and numbered lists to break down ideas
- Include short, well-defined paragraphs
- Embed relevant statistics and cited sources when possible
- Ensure each page has a clear topic and stays on that subject

✅ Establishing Authority and Credibility

- Write About pages and bios that clearly state your expertise
- Reference your unique frameworks, processes, or systems
- Maintain a consistent message across all public platforms
- Get mentioned or linked on high-authority platforms (LinkedIn, Medium, Quora, Wikipedia)
- Encourage third-party reviews and testimonials on trusted platforms

✅ Technical Optimization

- Use structured data and schema markup to define entities
- Submit your sitemap to Google Search Console
- Optimize internal links for semantic clarity and context
- Make sure your site is mobile friendly and loads fast
- Use alt text on all images to increase context for AI crawlers

✅ Platform Presence and Distribution

- Repurpose blog content into YouTube videos, podcasts, and Substack posts
- Engage on AI-indexed platforms like Reddit, LinkedIn, and Quora
- Submit guest articles to reputable blogs or digital magazines
- Publish audio or video transcripts for LLMs to index
- Keep Google My Business, Yelp, and Trustpilot profiles active and up to date

✅ AI-Specific Engagement and Monitoring

- Test your business visibility with prompts in ChatGPT, Claude, and Perplexity

- Build and deploy your own custom GPT or AI assistant trained on your content
- Analyze assistant conversations to understand common questions and gaps
- Monitor brand mentions with tools like Brand24 or Talkwalker
- Track traffic coming from AI-powered tools and platforms

✅ **Content Quality and Clarity**

- Avoid filler and fluff—focus on depth and specificity
- Use a clear call to action on every page or piece
- Align your content with real user problems and outcomes
- Audit content with tools like ChatGPT or Frase for clarity and optimization
- Continually update content to stay accurate and current

12

Prompt Library: Content Optimization with ChatGPT

Content Planning and Topic Discovery

Prompt 1:

What questions are people asking about [insert your industry/topic] that are not being answered well online?

Prompt 2:

Give me 10 blog post titles that would rank well in AI-generated answers for someone searching for [insert solution or topic].

Prompt 3:

What are the most common problems business owners face when trying to [insert service you offer]?

Prompt 4:

Act like a customer looking for [insert service]. What kind of questions would they ask ChatGPT?

Content Drafting and Formatting

Prompt 5:

Write a blog post outline that would be easy for AI tools to understand and reference for the topic [insert topic]. Include clear sections and bullet points.

Prompt 6:

Rewrite this paragraph so it's easier for an AI assistant to summarize and reference in a response: [insert paragraph].

Prompt 7:

Turn this content into a question-and-answer format that an AI could pull from to answer user questions. Use clear headings and bullet points.

Prompt 8:

Format the following content so it aligns with how AI tools prefer to read and extract data: [insert article or blog].

Content Optimization and Clarity

Prompt 9:

Analyze this content and give me suggestions to improve clarity, structure, and keyword relevance: [insert blog post or paragraph].

Prompt 10:

Does this content answer a user's question directly and clearly? If not, how can I improve it? [insert content]

Prompt 11:

Is this content likely to be referenced by AI tools? If not, how can I adjust the tone, format, or structure?

Creating Summaries, FAQs, and Featured Snippets

Prompt 12:

Summarize this article into 3 bullet points that could be used as a featured answer by an AI assistant. [insert article]

Prompt 13:

Generate a list of FAQs and answers based on the following content. [insert content]

Prompt 14:

Create a concise summary of this blog post that AI tools could reference in a paragraph: [insert blog post]

Content Repurposing for AI-Indexed Platforms

Prompt 15:

Turn this blog post into a Reddit-style answer for a question about [insert topic]. Keep it clear and helpful. [insert blog post]

Prompt 16:

Convert this blog into a LinkedIn post that showcases authority and encourages engagement. [insert content]

Prompt 17:

Rewrite this blog post as a script for a short YouTube video. Include a hook, main points, and call to action. [insert blog post]

Prompt 18:

Summarize this podcast transcript into a LinkedIn article that could be picked up by AI tools. [insert transcript]

Testing Your Visibility

Prompt 19:

If someone asked ChatGPT, "Who are the top experts in [your industry]?" would I show up based on this content? Analyze and suggest improvements. [insert bio or article]

Prompt 20:

What AI-friendly platforms should I publish this content on to increase the chances it will be used in AI answers?

Prompt 21:

What else can I add to this piece to increase its chances of being cited by ChatGPT, Claude, or Perplexity? [insert content]

13

AIO Audit Worksheet

Objective: Assess your current digital presence and content to determine how AI-friendly and visible your business is.

Section 1: Foundational Visibility

1.1 Business Clarity

- Is your business clearly described on your website, LinkedIn, and About pages?
- Do your bios and elevator pitches use the same language your customers would use in AI queries?
- Do you have a consistent brand voice across all platforms?

1.2 Unique Authority

- Do you mention proprietary methods, frameworks, or expertise that AI can associate with your brand?
- Is your leadership team mentioned by name on trusted platforms or cited as experts?
- Are your credentials, affiliations, or achievements clearly listed?

Section 2: Content Strategy and Structure

2.1 Content Relevance

- Do your blog posts, videos, or podcast episodes answer real questions your target audience asks?
- Are topics aligned with natural language queries, not just keyword-focused?

2.2 Formatting for AI

- Are your articles structured with H1, H2, and H3 headers?
- Do you use bullet points, numbered lists, and bolded key phrases to guide AI comprehension?
- Are summaries and FAQs included in your long-form content?

Section 3: Platform Reach

3.1 AI-Indexed Platforms

- Do you actively post on LinkedIn, Reddit, Medium, Quora, or other high-visibility platforms?
- Have you created content on YouTube, Substack, or in podcasts where transcripts are available?
- Are you cited or quoted on third-party sites like Wikipedia, Yelp, or news outlets?

3.2 Review Signals and Mentions

- Do you have current and consistent reviews on platforms like Google My Business, Trustpilot, or industry directories?
- Have you monitored where your brand or name appears across AI-powered tools using alerts or brand monitoring software?

Section 4: Technical Foundations

4.1 Site Optimization

- Does your site use structured data and schema markup?
- Is your sitemap submitted and indexed by Google?
- Do your images have alt text and descriptive filenames?

4.2 AI Readiness

- Have you trained a custom GPT or assistant with your business FAQs or knowledge base?
- Are you testing prompts in ChatGPT, Claude, and Perplexity to see how often your business is mentioned?

Section 5: Content Performance and Feedback

5.1 Engagement Tracking

- Are you using heatmaps or behavior tracking tools to measure engagement on high-performing content?
- Do you monitor time on page and bounce rates for key blog posts or service pages?

5.2 Feedback Collection

- Do you ask visitors how they found you, including whether they used an AI tool?
- Have you gathered feedback on whether your content answered their questions clearly and completely?

Section 6: Repurposing and Distribution

6.1 Content Repurposing

- Do you transform blog posts into video scripts, infographics, or podcast topics?
- Are transcripts available and searchable for video or audio content?

6.2 Syndication Strategy

- Do you share your content across different platforms to increase AI indexing?
- Are you mentioned or quoted on partner websites or guest blogs?

Scoring and Action Plan

Score each item from 1 to 5:

1 = Not in place

3 = In progress or partially optimized

5 = Fully optimized

Total Score: ________ / 120

Areas of Strength: ______________________________________

Areas to Improve: ______________________________________

Top 3 Next Steps:

14

Glossary of AIO Terms

AIO (AI Optimization)

The practice of optimizing your digital presence, content, and brand so that it is visible, relevant, and referenced by AI tools like ChatGPT, Claude, Gemini, and Perplexity. Similar in intent to SEO, but designed for large language models rather than traditional search engines.

LLM (Large Language Model)

A type of AI trained on massive amounts of text data that can understand, generate, and summarize human language. Examples include ChatGPT, Claude, and Gemini. LLMs are used to power conversational search and AI-generated answers.

AI-Crawled Platforms

Websites and tools whose content is frequently indexed or referenced by AI tools. These include Reddit, Quora, Medium, Wikipedia, LinkedIn, and major news publications. Publishing on these platforms increases your likelihood of being cited in AI responses.

Semantic Relevance

The alignment between the intent of a user's question and the meaning of your content. AI tools prioritize content that matches user intent, even if it doesn't contain exact keywords.

Evergreen Content

Content that remains relevant over time. These are topics and answers that do not expire quickly and are likely to be referenced repeatedly by AI tools and search engines.

Featured Answer / AI Citation

A short, high-authority excerpt that AI tools highlight when answering a user's query. Similar to a featured snippet in SEO, but driven by how well your content aligns with AI's understanding of the question.

AIO-Optimized Content

Content that is structured, formatted, and written in a way that makes it easy for AI tools to read, understand, and reference. Includes headings, summaries, bullet points, and clear answers to likely user questions.

LLM Behavior

The way large language models make decisions about which content to use. Key behaviors include semantic matching, hallucination risk (producing inaccurate answers), and token memory (limited content recall within a single session).

Prompt Engineering

The process of crafting effective questions or instructions for AI tools to produce useful, relevant, or optimized responses. In AIO, prompts are used to audit content, generate ideas, and test visibility.

AI-Friendly Formatting

The practice of structuring content so that it is easy for AI tools to scan, parse, and summarize. This includes the use of headlines, subheadings, concise paragraphs, lists, and structured data.

Digital Footprint

The collection of all your online content and brand mentions across platforms. A strong digital footprint increases your visibility in AI-generated answers.

Custom GPT / Branded Assistant

A personalized AI tool built on platforms like ChatGPT that is trained on your business knowledge, FAQs, and content. Used for lead generation, customer service, or internal knowledge delivery.

AIO Audit

A structured review of your business's digital content and presence to assess how well it is optimized for AI visibility. Includes evaluating structure, authority, clarity, and platform distribution.

Authority Signals

Indicators that AI uses to determine whether your content is trustworthy and credible. These include reviews, testimonials, external citations, and your history of publishing valuable content.

LLM-Trainable Content

Content that is created in such a way that AI tools can easily learn from it. This includes About pages, team bios, FAQ sections, and process descriptions that clearly define your business and its value.

Content Summarization

AI's ability to distill large volumes of text into concise summaries. To appear in summaries, your content must be well-organized, specific, and aligned with common user intent.

AI-Indexed Platforms

Websites and content repositories that AI tools frequently pull data from. Publishing regularly on these platforms increases the chances that your business will appear in AI answers.

www.ingramcontent.com/pod-product-compliance
Lightning Source LLC
LaVergne TN
LVHW022005200926
848481LV00007B/2239
* 9 7 9 8 2 3 1 1 8 4 9 5 8 *